CONTENTS

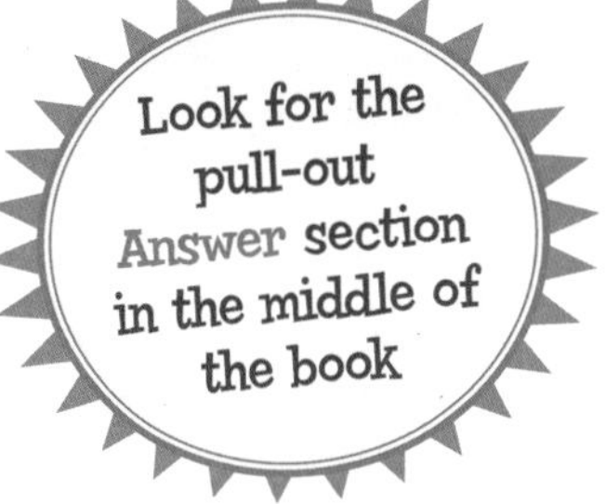
Look for the pull-out Answer section in the middle of the book

HOW TO USE THIS BOOK

The **Targeting Grammar 3** activity book provides basic instruction in grammar for Year 3 students. It explains the 'parts of speech' — the types of words that make up our language — such as nouns, pronouns, adjectives, verbs and adverbs. It features a section for each, which contain the following:

- **Essentials** — included at the beginning, these pages summarise the main elements of each part of speech and provide examples.
- **Activities** — parts of speech are explored through a variety of activities to ensure that students have grasped the learning before moving on to the next idea.
- **Challenges** — activities appear throughout the sections to allow students to extend themselves through more complex and longer-form questioning.
- **Checkpoints** — assessment written to review students' understanding and consolidate their knowledge of the topic. Checkpoints also enable teachers and parents to monitor progress and intervene where necessary.
- **Reading and Writing activities** — encourage students to apply their learning in narrative form. These activities provide imaginative stimulus and opportunities for analysis.
- **Punctuation stops** — include useful advice on how to correctly use punctuation marks in their writing. This ensures that students understand the fundamental punctuation concepts that relate to correct use of grammar.

A pull-out section containing the answers for all activities is included in the centre of the book.

About the author

Del has enjoyed a long career in education as a specialist teacher (Learning Difficulties), education adviser and regional coordinator (English). She has written extensively for parents, teachers and students, and is a well-known and respected author nationally and internationally. Her publications cover a diverse range of print and electronic materials in English grammar, spelling, reading, writing and comprehension.

Among her latest works are **Blake's Grammar & Punctuation Guide** and **Targeting Spelling**, a comprehensive spelling program.

NOUNS: Essentials

We express our thoughts in words. We put the words together in 'chunks' of meaning called **sentences**. We express ourselves thought by thought, sentence by sentence. Each thought connects to the one before it.

Each word in a sentence has a job to do. In this section, you will learn about the words that name what is in our world: the people, the places and the things. These naming words are called **nouns**. There are different types of nouns.

People use words to talk to each other. When we write, we put a small space between words to show where they begin and end, like this:

Jackplaysfootballatweekends.

Jack plays football at weekends.

✤ TYPES OF NOUNS

	Examples
Common nouns name *people*, *places*, *animals* and *things*.	man, girl, tiger, dog, shop, school, book, cup
Concrete nouns name the things we can *see* and *touch*.	cup, pizza, book, medal, prize
Abstract nouns name *thoughts* and *feelings*. We cannot see or touch them.	love, joy, freedom, anger
Compound nouns are made up of *two word parts*.	**cow**boy, **foot**ball, **sea**shell
Proper nouns are the *special names* given to people, places and things. A **capital letter** is required at the beginning of each word.	**K**athy, **P**erth, **A**ustralia, **W**oolworths, **B**risbane **R**iver, **O**lympic **G**ames, **E**aster

Singular and plural nouns	*Examples*
Singular nouns name *one* thing.	bat, plane, animal, ticket, brush
Plural nouns name *more than one* thing. Most plural nouns are made by adding **-s** or **-es** to the singular noun.	bats, planes, animals, tickets, brushes boy, boy**s**; tree, tree**s**; dish, dish**es**; fox, fox**es**
Count nouns name things that *can* be counted.	apples, horses, books, cars
Mass nouns name things that *cannot* be counted. Mass nouns are always **singular**.	rice, sugar, sand, snow, rain *Rain* falls from clouds. *Snow* is white.
Possessive nouns show ownership. An **apostrophe** is required before or after the **s**.	Jill**'s** hat, foxes**'** tails
Collective nouns name groups of things. Each group has members.	herd, crowd, flock *herd* of cows, *crowd* of people, *flock* of sheep

✤ NOUN GROUPS

A **noun group** is a group of words built around a **key noun**. It usually begins with an article (or other determiner) and can contain other words. The noun is the main word in the group.

Determiners	*Examples*
A **determiner** is part of a **noun group**. Its job is to *point out* (determine) the noun. Determiners include all **possessive nouns**, and words such as **my**, **its**, **your**, **their**, **some** and **each**.	*the* book, *my* blue hat, *Jim's* football, *her* sister's friend, *some* bad apples
Articles are also determiners. They often introduce a noun group.	a, an, the
A (or **an**) is an **indefinite article**. It comes before a singular noun. **An** is used when the next word begins with a vowel.	*a* horse, *a* tree, *an* egg, *an* old man
The is a **definite article** and points to something *particular* or *definite*. It is used before singular and plural nouns.	*the* sun, *the* moon, *the* last page, *the* cow in *the* paddock

When you see this sign, you can decide whether you want to challenge yourself!

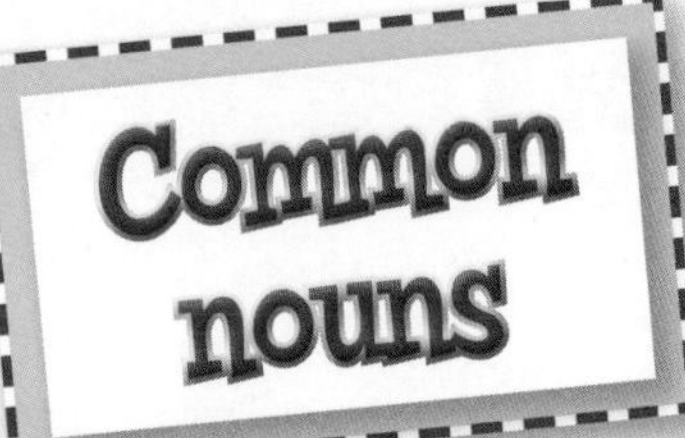
Common nouns

Common nouns name the *everyday things* in our world — the people, places, animals and things, e.g. man, zebra, coat, shop.

1 Add three more common nouns to each list.

People	Places	Animals	Things
teacher	park	crocodile	chair
actor	circus	elephant	computer
soldier	beach	lizard	stove
______	______	______	______
______	______	______	______
______	______	______	______

2 Add a common noun to complete each sentence.

Molly ate a ______________.

Nat has a pet ______________.

I like to play ______________.

Go and sit by the ______________.

I saw Jill at the ______________.

Common nouns name everyday things.

3 Choose the best common noun to match each picture.

house castle shed	yacht ship canoe	shoes boots slippers	street lane road

TARGETING GRAMMAR 3 © PASCAL PRESS ISBN 9781925076592

Circle only the common nouns in the box. Choose one to complete each sentence.

monkey	shut	lightning	pretty	bush
read	dragon	lazy	kick	calf

The children became lost in the ________________.

________________ flashed across the sky.

This book is about a knight and a ________________.

The baby ________________ stood on her thin, wobbly legs.

The chattering ________________ swung from branch to branch.

NOUNS

Name five common nouns you would see in these places.

Under the sea	In the sky	In a garden

Highlight ten different common nouns in this report.

An emu is a large Australian bird that cannot fly. It is about two metres tall and has a long, thin neck and light brown feathers. The emu has strong, powerful legs, so it can run very fast. Emus eat flowers, seeds, lizards and large insects — especially caterpillars.

The female lays between seven and twenty eggs in a nest on the ground. The chicks are brown and white when they hatch, so they are well hidden in the grass. Emus can live for up to twenty years.

NOUNS

**Read some facts about volcanoes. Draw a diagram and label it using common nouns from the text below.
Write a caption below the diagram.**

VOLCANOES

Across the world, there are many mountains that sometimes explode and send steam, ash and rocks high into the air. These mountains are called **volcanoes**. The word 'volcano' comes from *Vulcan*, the ancient Roman God of Fire.

Below a volcano, there is a pool of hot liquid rock called **lava**. Sometimes, steam and gas force the liquid up through an opening that leads to the Earth's surface. The pressure can be so great that the volcano **erupts**, sending clouds of ash and hot rocks high into the air through the hole at the top. This hole is called a **crater**.

TARGETING GRAMMAR 3 © PASCAL PRESS ISBN 9781925076592

Concrete and abstract nouns

Common nouns are either **concrete** or **abstract**. **Concrete nouns** name the things we can *see*, *hear* or *touch*, e.g. book, car, thunder, pizza, prickle. **Abstract nouns** name *feelings*, e.g. joy, happiness, fear. They also name *ideas*, e.g. hope, bravery, curiosity.

NOUNS

In the boxes, write C beside the concrete nouns and A beside the abstract nouns.

	love		emu		sadness		insect		rice
	bucket		joy		power		anger		violin
	fear		broom		pride		soup		beauty

Tick whether the nouns are concrete or abstract.

	Concrete	Abstract
The boys trembled in **fear**.		✓
Mum said we must be home by **nightfall**.		
The truck driver shouted in **anger**.		
I left with tears in my eyes and **sorrow** in my heart.		
This story is about missing pirate **treasure**.		
He stared at the broken bat in **amazement**.		

Circle the abstract nouns in these sentences.

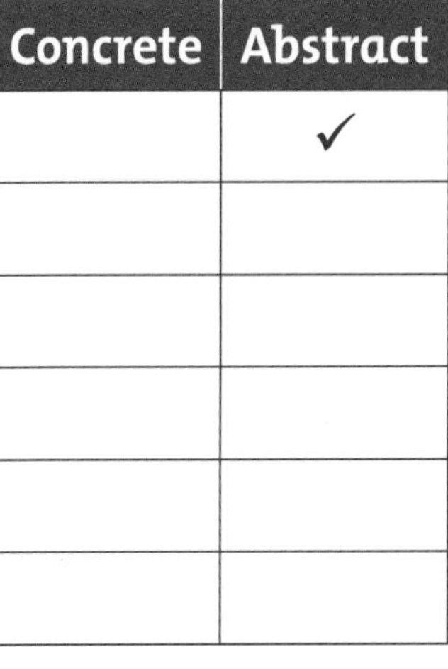

There was great excitement when our team won the game.

The people are fighting for their freedom.

His face was red with embarrassment.

The soldier received a medal for his bravery.

Sara stood before the class and spoke with confidence.

Abstract nouns name feelings and ideas.

Choose one of these abstract nouns and use it to write a sentence.

sleep   luck   success

NOUNS

1. **Circle the abstract nouns in this text.**

It was Christmas morning. Zac bounded down the stairs in great excitement. His mum smiled with pleasure and handed him a large, bulky gift. "Happy Christmas, Zac," she said.
Full of curiosity, Zac tore off the wrapping. He stared in amazement. In his hands was a shiny new skateboard.
"What a wonderful surprise! Thanks, Mum," Zac said, and he danced around the room in great delight.

2. **Write a poem using these abstract nouns to show your feelings. Add illustrations.**

Happiness is a chocolate cake.

Sadness is the loss of a toy.

Embarrassment is a red face and shaky knees.

Fear is ....

....

Love is ....

....

Kindness is ....

....

Pride is ....

....

Friendship is ....

....

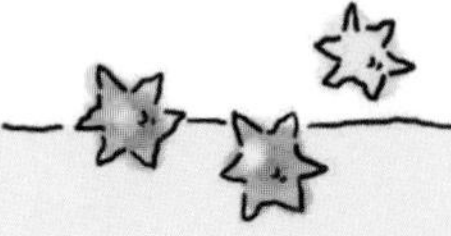

TARGETING GRAMMAR 3 © PASCAL PRESS ISBN 9781925076592

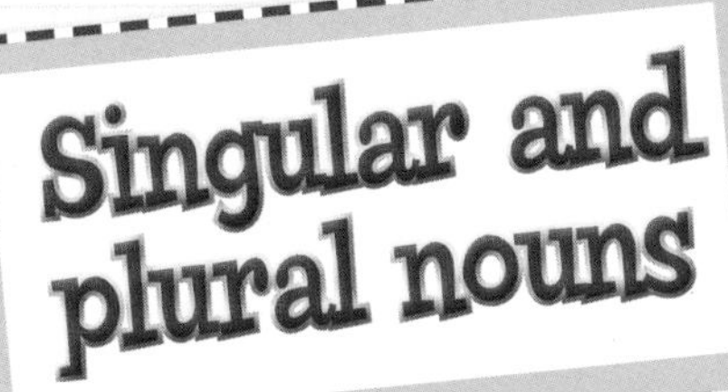

A **singular noun** names *one thing*.
A **plural noun** names *more than one thing*.
To make a noun **plural**, add **-s** or **-es**, e.g. cow, cow**s**; stick, stick**s**; box, box**es**.

Write the plural forms of these nouns.

ball	________	koala	________
plate	________	peach	________
fox	________	game	________
brush	________	dress	________

NOUNS

Add a plural ending to the nouns.

The **boy**___ and **girl**___ are building a big sandcastle.

I bought five **apple**___, two **peach**___ and four **banana**___.

Those **box**___ are filled with **bottle**___ of plum jam.

We saw **lion**___, **tiger**___ and **ostrich**___ at the zoo.

Put your **book**___ on the shelf and your **toy**___ in the toy box.

Count and mass nouns

Things that *can* be counted are **count nouns**. They have a **singular** and **plural** form, e.g. dog**s**, friend**s**, dish**es**.
Things that *can't* be counted are **mass nouns** and are always **singular**, e.g. wheat, sugar, bread.

Use a red pencil to circle the mass nouns.

A mass noun is always followed by a singular verb.

rain	biscuit	coffee	peanut	storm	snow	
tomato	milk	letter	koala	butter	lollipop	oil
cream	turtle	leaf	tea	jelly	vinegar	honey

Some nouns have a special **plural form**, e.g. foot, **feet**; man, **men**.

4 Write the plural form of each noun that appears in brackets.

Some of the [child] are wearing hats. ____________

Clean your [tooth] after each meal. ____________

The [woman] are shopping for shoes. ____________

The farmer has a duck and two [goose]. ____________

There are [mouse] in the barn. ____________

Nouns ending in y
If the letter before **y** is a vowel, add **s**. Examples: boy, boy**s**; key, key**s**
If the letter before **y** is *not* a vowel, change **y** to **i** and add **es**.
Examples: body, bod**ies**; lady, lad**ies**

5 Spot the spelling mistake in each sentence.
Underline the mistake and write it correctly on the line.

Mothers are carrying their babys. ____________

The jockies rode their horses past the post. ____________

Sara has travelled to many countrys. ____________

There are seven dayes in a week. ____________

White daisys grow in my garden. ____________

Nouns ending in f or fe
If you hear an **f** sound in the plural, just add **s**.
Examples: roof, roof**s**; chief, chief**s**
If you hear a **v** sound in the plural, change **f** to **v** and add **es**.
Examples: loaf, loa**ves**; knife, kni**ves**

6 Write the nouns from the box in their plural forms.

leaf	All the ____________ have fallen from the tree.
calf	The cows and their ____________ are in the yard.
cliff	There was a sandy beach below the steep ____________.
shelf	The supermarket ____________ are stocked with food.
roof	Most of the ____________ in my street are painted red.

Proper nouns are the special *names* given to people, places and things. They begin with a **capital letter**, e.g. **W**illiam, **F**riday, **A**pril, **C**hristmas, **A**ustralia.

NOUNS

1 Write some proper nouns. Don't forget to start with a capital letter.

A boy's name beginning with **h** ______________

A city beginning with **s** ______________

A country beginning with **a** ______________

A day beginning with **t** ______________

A month beginning with **j** ______________

The name of a river ______________

The name of a shop ______________

The name of a pet ______________

2 Give the proper nouns a big capital letter.

sam has an internet penpal who lives in africa. His name is kudzi. kudzi lives in a town called addo, beside the vaal river. sam and kudzi both love to play soccer. One day, kudzi would like to visit sam in australia.

3 Choose a proper noun for each common noun.

car	Pepsi	chocolate	Victoria
drink	English	movie	Thomas
day	Toyota	state	Snickers
subject	Thursday	boy	Batman

Proper nouns are the special names of people, places and things.

4 Write one or two sentences about the Olympic Games.

____

____

____

____

  ISBN 9781925076592

Circle the proper names in this recount then answer the questions.

On Sunday, my sister Helen and I went to the Queensland Museum in Brisbane.

There were lots of interesting things to see. We liked the dinosaurs best of all.

Later, we went for a ride on the Brisbane Wheel. This ferris wheel was put at South Bank about six years ago. From high in the air, we could see all over the city of Brisbane. It was very exciting.

We walked through the Grand Arbour in the South Bank Parklands. This walkway is one kilometre long and is covered in purple flowers.

We had a picnic lunch beside the Brisbane River. In the afternoon, we went across the river on a CityCat. The name of this ferry is *The Spirit of Brisbane*.

(i) What is my sister's name? ....

(ii) What place did we visit first? ....

(iii) What is the ferris wheel called? ....

(iv) Where is the Grand Arbour? ....

(v) What is the name of the river? ....

TARGETING GRAMMAR 3 © PASCAL PRESS ISBN 9781925076592

CHALLENGE

1 **Use a big capital letter to mark the proper nouns in this recount.**

We have a new boy in our class. His name is sahil. He came from india with his mum and dad, and his sister simran. They arrived in december, just after christmas day.

His father is going to teach at bedford university. I think sahil and I will be great friends because we both love to play cricket.

NOUNS

2 **Highlight the words that need a capital letter in this biography.**

Alice in Wonderland is one of the most famous children's books in the world. it was written by charles dodgson under the pen-name of lewis carroll and was published almost 150 years ago.

charles dodgson was born in england in 1832. he liked to entertain his family with magic tricks, poetry and puppet shows. at the age of 24, he was a teacher of maths at oxford university.

one summer, the liddell family came to stay. dodgson entertained the children by telling them stories about a girl called alice, who fell down a rabbit hole and had exciting adventures in an underground world. the stories were full of strange and comical characters, such as the mad hatter, the queen of hearts, tweedledee and tweedledum, and the white rabbit — who was always late!

dodgson later made the story into a book, called *Alice's Adventures in Wonderland*. the illustrations were done by a friend of his and are almost as famous as the stories.

Remember that sentences always begin with a capital letter.

TARGETING GRAMMAR 3 © PASCAL PRESS ISBN 9781925076592

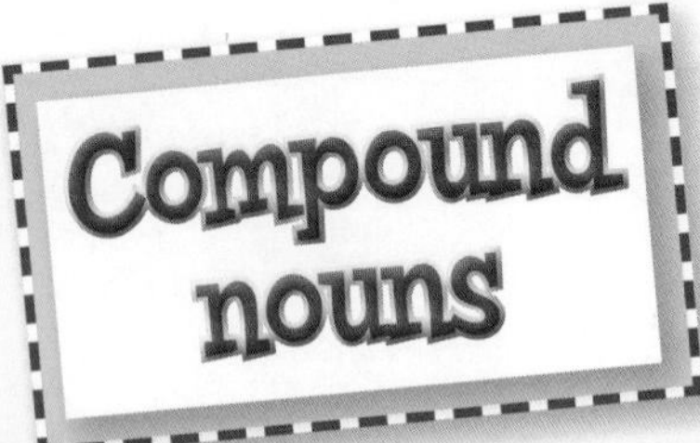
Compound nouns

Some nouns are made up of *two words*. These are called **compound nouns**.
moon + light = moonlight
cow + boy = cowboy milk + shake = milkshake

Illustrate these compound nouns.

butterfly	surfboard	sunglasses	scarecrow	lighthouse

Join two nouns to make compound nouns.

sun	way	day	ground
path	brush	sports	belt
tooth	hive	snake	light
bee	shine	seat	bite

Write a sentence about (i) pancakes and (ii) sandcastles.

(i) ______________________

(ii) ______________________

Build these compound nouns.

sea — shell seashell
sea — weed ______
sea — side ______
sea — food ______

sea — shore ______
sea — horse ______
sea — gull ______
sea — bed ______

Highlight the compound nouns in each sentence.

I found a horseshoe in the haystack.
A dragonfly was caught in a cobweb.
He ran down the footpath to the boatshed.
There are twelve doughnuts in the cardboard box.
We rode on horseback to the waterfall.

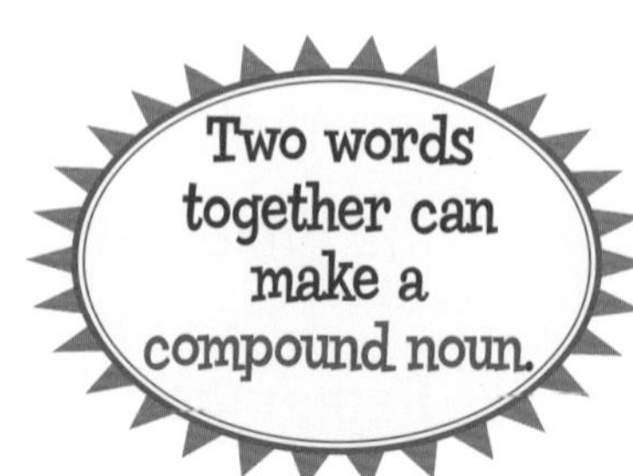
Two words together can make a compound noun.

NOUNS

TARGETING GRAMMAR 3 © PASCAL PRESS ISBN 9781925076592

Collective nouns

A **collective noun** names a *group*, e.g. army, team, herd, pride.
The group has *members*, e.g. an **army** of men, a **team** of players, a **herd** of goats, a **pride** of lions.

1 **Choose a collective noun from the box to complete each sentence.**

flock	herd	pod	mob	swarm

A __________ of kangaroos is drinking at the waterhole.

The dog ran around the __________ of cows.

There was a __________ of bees around the beehive.

A __________ of seagulls flew over the fishing boats.

A __________ of whales swam slowly up the coast.

2 **Match the groups and their members.**

litter	sheep	crowd	elephants
pack	flies	shoal	chickens
flock	kittens	brood	people
cloud	wolves	herd	fish

3 **Add a collective noun to each sentence. Choose from the words in the list.**

He is captain of the football __________.

There is a __________ of books on the top shelf.

I gave mum a __________ of roses.

The kite landed in a __________ of trees.

If we had a __________ of cards, we could play Snap.

pack
bunch
team
clump
stack

A collective noun names a group of people or things.

1 **Write a paragraph about a team you have played in. Illustrate your text.**

2 **Under each picture, write the correct collective noun from the text.**

I live on a farm with my mum and dad. In our hayshed, there is a nest of mice living up in the rafters. Below, on the soft straw, is our cat, Bessie. She is watching over her new litter of tiny kittens. Outside, a hen and her brood of chicks are scratching on the ground for seeds.

In one paddock, we have a flock of sheep. Dad keeps a careful eye on them because a pack of wild dogs sometimes roams through the hills. We have a large herd of cows, which are brought in for milking twice a day.

TARGETING GRAMMAR 3 © PASCAL PRESS ISBN 9781925076592

Possessive nouns

Some nouns show *ownership*. These are **possessive nouns**. An **apostrophe (')** is used to show who the owner is.

Singular

For a **singular noun** owner, add **'s**, e.g. Jack**'s** dog, Dad**'s** car, the cat**'s** tail.

To show ownership, add 's to a singular noun.

NOUNS

1 Write the singular possessive nouns.

Mum has a handbag. It is Mum's handbag.

Sally has a bike. It is __________ bike.

The dog has a collar. It is the __________ collar.

My teacher has many books. They are my __________ books.

His uncle has a horse. It is his __________ horse.

A bird has feathers. They are the __________ feathers.

2 Who is the owner of the things that are underlined?

I patted my friend's <u>dog</u>. __________

Jeremy's <u>house</u> is next to mine. __________

The fisherman's <u>hat</u> blew away. __________

An emu's <u>legs</u> are long and strong. __________

There are cows in the farmer's <u>paddock</u>. __________

3 Write a sentence about (i) a bird's cage and (ii) a spider's web.

(i) __________

(ii) __________

4 Change the noun in the box to a possessive noun.

dog baby sailor Sue butterfly

He stepped on the __________ tail.

A teddy bear sits beside the __________ cot.

The __________ hat is black and white.

__________ coat is thick and warm.

A __________ wings are very colourful.

TARGETING GRAMMAR 3 © PASCAL PRESS ISBN 9781925076592

Most **plural nouns** end in **-s**. To show *ownership*, just add an **apostrophe**, e.g. cat**s'** claws, bird**s'** feathers, the lion**s'** den, the boy**s'** bikes.

5 Name the owners of the items in bold.

They found dinosaurs' **bones** in the pit. ____________

The jockeys' **horses** are young and fast. ____________

Miss Dee took a photo of her students' **work**. ____________

The athletes' **uniforms** are green and gold. ____________

The boys' **torches** lit up the cave. ____________

6 Tick whether the possessive nouns are singular or plural.

	Singular	Plural
Emily's hat is made of straw.		
This shop sells ladies' shoes.		
Water sparkled on spiders' webs.		
Dad's reading glasses are on the table.		
Magpies' nests are made of twigs, sticks and grass.		

7 Tick the correct sentence in each pair.

Only possessive nouns need an apostrophe. Don't confuse them with plural nouns!

- [ ] The trucks are loaded with hay.
- [ ] The truck's are loaded with hay.

- [ ] A butterfly's wings are colourful.
- [ ] A butterflies wings are colourful.

- [ ] Water ran off the duck's back.
- [ ] Water ran off the ducks back.

- [ ] A foxes tail is long and bushy.
- [ ] A fox's tail is long and bushy.

To show ownership, put an apostrophe after most plural nouns.

TARGETING GRAMMAR 3 © PASCAL PRESS ISBN 9781925076592

1 **Add apostrophes to the underlined nouns to show ownership.**

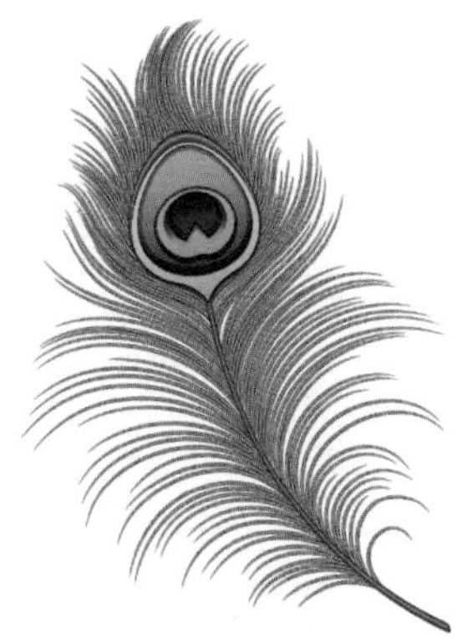

A fisherman stands at the <u>waters</u> edge.
All the <u>kids</u> bikes are in the bike rack.
A <u>giraffes</u> neck is very long.
Jason collects <u>birds</u> feathers.
It is hard to read <u>Tims</u> writing.

2 **Circle the possessive nouns in this text.**

Ashar and Tom have horses. Ashar's horse is black and Tom's horse is chestnut. The boys like to ride across the farmer's field to an old shepherd's hut perched on the river's edge. They tie up their horses and go looking for birds' nests and spiders' webs. Once they saw a fox's burrow. Today they hoped to find some turtles' eggs, but all they saw was a duck's feather.

3 **Use an apostrophe to mark the possessive nouns.**

NOUNS

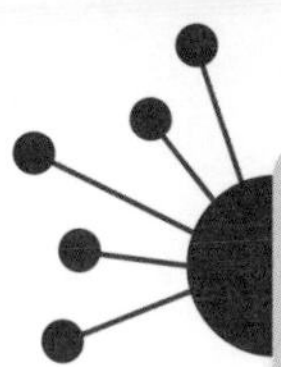

Punctuation stop

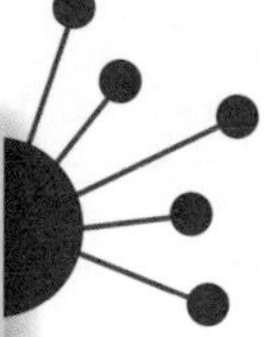

Writers mark their text to help readers make meaning. These marks are called **punctuation marks**.

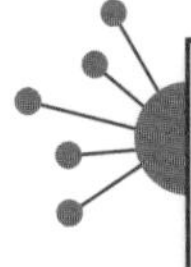

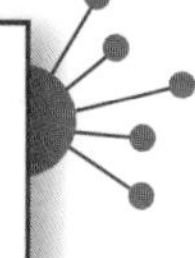

A **Capital letters** are used for *proper names* and to mark the *beginning of a sentence*.

• A **full stop** marks the *end of a sentence*.

1 Use a red pencil to mark the capital letters and full stops.

one of australia's best-known bush poets is 'banjo' paterson he was born more than 150 years ago and grew up in country new south wales he went to a school in sydney and later worked at a law firm

one of his best-known poems is *The Man from Snowy River* he also wrote the words of the famous song *waltzing matilda* his face appears on the australian $10 note

Commas show readers when to take a *short break* between words.
They are used to separate **nouns** in a *list*,
e.g. I like apples, bananas, oranges and pears.

2 Use a red pencil to add the missing commas.

Oranges lemons and limes are all citrus fruits.

The farmer keeps horses cows pigs ducks and hens.

Wheat sugar coal and iron ore are exported to Asia.

Dairy products include milk cheese butter and yoghurt.

Jill's three best friends are Sue Judy and Carol.

TARGETING GRAMMAR 3 © PASCAL PRESS ISBN 9781925076592

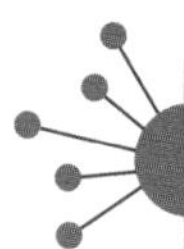

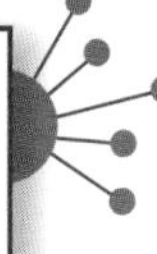

Apostrophes are used with **nouns** to show *ownership*.
Add **'s** to **singular nouns**,
e.g. the boy**'s** bike, the girl**'s** hat.
Add an **apostrophe (')** after the **s** to most **plural nouns**,
e.g. the boy**s'** bikes, the girl**s'** hats.

3 **Add apostrophes to show ownership in these sentences.**

Jerry washed his dads car.

A giraffes neck is very long.

All the students hats are blue.

Jen rode her sisters bike to school.

Sharks teeth are razor sharp.

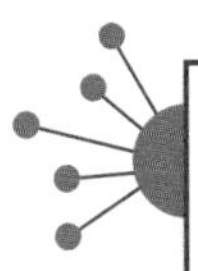

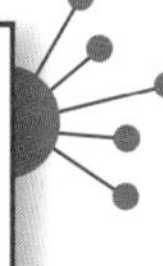

Apostrophes are also used to *shorten* words.
These words are called **contractions**,
e.g. do not = don't, did not = didn't, she is = she's,
I have = I've

4 **Match these words to their shortened forms.**

does not	couldn't	he is	I'm
have not	hasn't	you are	he's
was not	doesn't	we had	they've
could not	haven't	I am	we'd
has not	wasn't	they have	you're

5 **Write a contraction for the words written in the brackets.**

He [is not] at school yet. ____________

[We have] never been to China. ____________

They [were not] in the park. ____________

[It is] a very hot day. ____________

We [will not] go if it rains. ____________

Kerry [could not] find her puppy. ____________

Apostrophes have only two jobs to do!

TARGETING GRAMMAR 3 © PASCAL PRESS ISBN 9781925076592

Language is written in 'chunks' of meaning.
A **noun group** is a chunk of words *built around a noun.* All of the information in the chunk is about the **key noun**, e.g. a **cat**, a tabby **cat**, an old tabby **cat** by the fire.

Illustrate these noun groups.

a clown in baggy pants	a bunch of yellow flowers	a small black kitten	a girl with long blonde hair

Match the noun groups to the pictures.

a fox with a bushy tail

tiny black ants

a can of orange paint

a clown with a red nose

a basket of fruit

the long, thin snake

3 Expand these noun groups by adding more information about the noun.

a dog a wild dog

my hat ______

the moon ______

a dancer ______

the bike ______

the animals ______

Choose three of your expanded noun groups and build a sentence for each. Example: A wild dog is chasing the sheep.

(i) ______

(ii) ______

(iii) ______

TARGETING GRAMMAR 3 © PASCAL PRESS ISBN 9781925076592

Determiners

A **determiner** is part of a **noun group**. Its job is to *point out* (determine) the noun, e.g. **my** cat, **that** horse, **those** green ants, **some** red apples.

The **articles a** (**an**) and **the** are determiners often used to introduce a noun group.

Other determiners: this, that, these, those my, your, her, his, its, our, their some, both, each, every

Circle the determiners in these noun groups.

his cricket cap	their shoes	the sleepy owl
a broken plate	every week	her new bike
its sharp claws	some cheese	these marbles
each student	my best work	that old boat

Underline the noun groups built around the nouns that are bold.

We climbed that steep **mountain**.

The **boys** in my class play cricket.

My two best **friends** are Jill and Freda.

The chef made some sweet and creamy chocolate **puddings**.

Dark, grey **thunderclouds** rolled in over the city.

Those three black **horses** in the stable belong to Mrs Smith.

The is definite about what it names, e.g. the sun, the moon, the school captain.

A and an are used more generally, e.g. a book is any book; an apple is any apple.

Choose 'the', 'a' or 'an' to complete each sentence.

Gently place ________ egg in ________ pot of boiling water.

Look at ________ moon and ________ stars in ________ night sky.

He is ________ odd person, but ________ honest one.

Stir ________ stew then put ________ lid back on ________ saucepan.

Today, Mum made ________ apple pie and ________ batch of scones.

He is ________ oldest person in ________ team.

TARGETING GRAMMAR 3 © PASCAL PRESS ISBN 9781925076592

All **possessive nouns** are **determiners**. They show *ownership*, e.g. **Tom's** bike, **Mr Smith's** car, the **teacher's** books, the **dancers'** costumes.

 **Draw lines to match the noun groups and the pictures.**

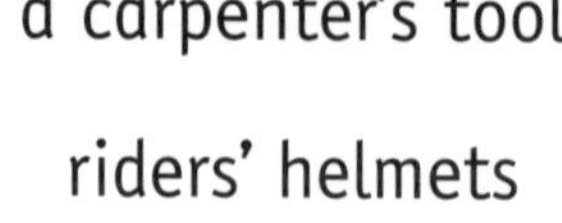

a carpenter's tool

riders' helmets

a chef's hat

Molly's ballet slippers

birds' feathers

the boy's kite

a man's red tie

a spider's web

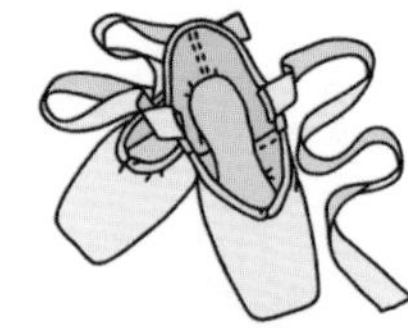

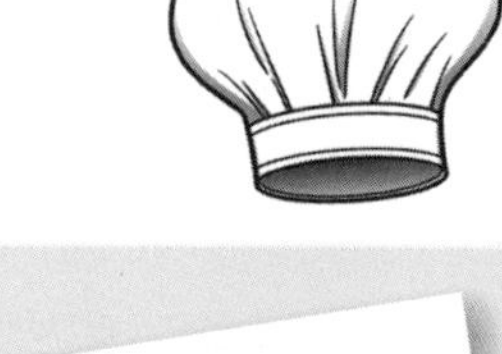

Joining word 'and'

A **noun group** may contain *two or more* nouns connected by **and**, which is known as a **joining word**, e.g. the boys **and** girls in my class; hot, buttered toast **and** jam; Jim **and** his friends; horses, cows, ducks **and** pigs; my socks **and** shoes.

 **Draw boxes around the noun groups in these sentences.**

I would enjoy [a glass of milk and a slice of cake.]

Did you see the lions, tigers and camels?

Jess and William will visit the museum and the art gallery.

The captain and his men marched down a long and dusty road.

I get emails and text messages on my mobile phone.

Tennis, hockey and basketball are my favourite sports.

Noun groups are important 'chunks' of language that help us to picture things clearly.

TARGETING GRAMMAR 3 © PASCAL PRESS ISBN 9781925076592

Read this short report about a carousel. Note how the noun groups give important details.

A CAROUSEL

A carousel is a ride for young children. It has a round platform that turns round and round. On the platform, there are some horses made of wood. They are painted in bright colours. Each horse has a saddle and a bridle, and stands on a wooden post.

A child sits on a horse, and someone pushes the carousel to make it go round and round. Some carousels have a motor that makes them go round and round. On some carousels, the horses move up and down, or rock backwards and forwards. Another name for a carousel is a merry-go-round.

Use the information in the noun groups to label the picture. Write a caption below the picture.

A carousel is ____________________

NOUNS

TARGETING GRAMMAR 3 © PASCAL PRESS ISBN 9781925076592

Nouns in Reading

In any text, the **nouns** tell you *who* and *what* you are reading about: the people, places and things. As you read, the information in the **noun groups** helps you to make pictures in your head and to understand what the writer is talking about.

Nouns are the keys that unlock meaning!

NOUNS

Highlight the noun groups in this story extract, then sketch the scene.

A huge wave rushed in from the sea. It smashed against the little sailing boat. It lifted it like a leaf in the wind. The mast broke and the boat was churned under the swirling water. The wave tossed the helpless boat against the sharp rocks and smashed it into splinters. The wave rolled back out to sea. The boat lay in pieces, scattered across the sand like matchsticks.

Nouns in Writing

When you are writing a text, use **noun groups** to talk about the people, places and things in your story. Remember, the **noun** is the main word in a noun group. The more information you include in the noun group, the easier it will be for your reader to picture the things you are writing about.

Write a short story in your notebook using the key nouns below. When you have finished, ask a friend to read it and draw a picture of your story.

team game goal winner

A capital letter begins a sentence.

A full stop ends a sentence.

Commas separate words in a list.

TARGETING GRAMMAR 3 © PASCAL PRESS ISBN 9781925076592

NOUNS Checkpoint ☑

Read this story extract. Circle five different common nouns.

Thick grey clouds are boiling and swirling over the top of Mount Shibar. Something warm brushes Pietro's cheek. Things begin falling from the sky. They feel like warm brown snowflakes ... and they are coming from the top of the mountain. The air is hard to breath and the clouds have come so low, he cannot see the sun.

Use a red pencil to give the proper nouns capital letters.

anzac day 2015 marked one hundred years since australian soldiers landed at gallipoli during world war I. Many australians attended a service at the australian war memorial in canberra to remember those who had fought there.

Are the bold nouns concrete or abstract? Mark the boxes with a C for concrete and an A for abstract.

☐ Her eyes lit up with **happiness**.

☐ Grandpa told us a tale about a talking **parrot**.

☐ Full of **curiosity**, the boys entered the stone cave.

☐ Jessica takes great **pride** in her work.

☐ I borrowed a book from the school **library**.

Write five compound nouns using the words below.

sports	shine	light	brush	seat
belt	tooth	sun	ground	house

____

NOUNS

5 Sort the nouns in the box into count nouns or mass nouns.

avocado	water	potato	sand	wheat
oil	storm	flower	cream	cloud

Count nouns	Mass nouns
____________	____________
____________	____________
____________	____________
____________	____________
____________	____________

6 Underline five noun groups in this text.

Pietro leads his donkey down the narrow mountain path to the fishing village of Mondova. He has baskets of olives and nuts, yellow cheeses, jars of olive oil, and crab pots woven by his father. He enters the crowded marketplace and finds his grandfather. He is already busy selling salted fish, grapes, juicy oranges and flat rounds of bread.

7 Punctuate this recount.

last saturday, it was toms ninth birthday he shouted with delight when he saw his dads present it was a little black and white puppy his mum gave him a shiny red skateboard when he opened his grans present, he found a book a game a toy truck and a box of chocolates tom said a happy thank you to all his family

TARGETING GRAMMAR 3 © PASCAL PRESS ISBN 9781925076592

PRONOUNS: Essentials

Substitute
(sub-stit-ute)
to take the place of

In this section, you will learn about words that can take the place of **nouns**.
These 'substitute' words are called **pronouns**.
The noun and its substitute pronoun must be the same in person and number.
This means:
Some pronouns replace **singular nouns**. (I, me, he, him, she, her)
Some pronouns replace **plural nouns**. (we, us, they, them)
Some pronouns replace the names of **males**. (he, him, they, them)
Some pronouns replace the names of **females**. (she, her, they, them)
Some pronouns replace the names of **things** that are neither male nor female. (it, they, them)
NOTE: The pronoun **you** can be either singular or plural, male or female.

✤ PRONOUNS

	Examples
Personal pronouns *replace* the names of people, places, animals and things.	**Ben** has two dogs. **He** *(Ben)* takes **them** *(the dogs)* for a walk every day. **Sarah** lost her hat in the park. **Mark** said that **he** *(Mark)* would help **her** *(Sarah)* look for **it** *(the hat)*. **He** *(Mark)* said that **it** *(the hat)* was bright red, so **they** *(Sarah and Mark)* should find **it** *(the hat)* easily.
Possessive pronouns *replace* **possessive nouns.** They never need an apostrophe.	This hat is **yours**. The books are **ours**. That horse is **mine**. The kitten is **hers**.
Reflexive pronouns *refer back* to the subject.	I hurt **myself**. He hit **himself**.
Some pronouns are used as **determiners** before nouns. (my, your, his, her, its, our, their)	**my** hat, **his** shoes, **our** friends, **their** lives
Interrogative pronouns are used to *ask questions*.	**Who** is the new teacher? **What** do you want? **Which** one is your bike?
Indefinite pronouns do not replace particular nouns. They refer to people and things in a *general way*.	**Everyone** has a ticket. I'd like **something** to eat. They lost **everything** in the fire.
Demonstrative pronouns point out *particular* people or things.	I saw **these** in a shop. Give **that** to your mum. Whose book is **this**? I like **those**.

Singular			Plural		
Personal	**Possessive**	**Reflexive**	**Personal**	**Possessive**	**Reflexive**
I me	mine	myself	we us	ours	ourselves
you	yours	yourself	you	yours	yourselves
she her	hers	herself	they them	theirs	themselves
he him	his	himself			
it	its	itself			

A **pronoun** usually follows the **noun** it replaces. A pronoun must refer clearly to the noun it replaces. This *pointing back* to a noun is called **pronoun reference.** It is very important because it ties ideas together. It helps to keep track of people and things in a text.

Example:
Hello, my name is Peter. My dog, Muffin, is a little Australian Terrier. She follows me everywhere. One sunny day, we were running in the park when a man and a black dog came jogging down the path. Muffin took off after them, yapping and snapping.

When you see this sign, you can decide whether you want to challenge yourself!

Personal pronouns

Pronouns *take the place* of **nouns**,
e.g. **Jim** had a **ball**. **He** lost **it** in the park.
(He = Jim, it = ball)

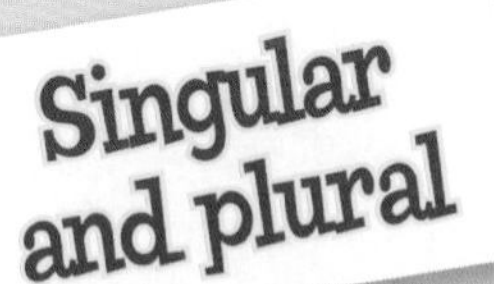

Singular pronouns replace singular nouns:
I me you he she it him her
Plural pronouns replace plural nouns:
we us you they them

1 Circle the personal pronouns in these sentences.

The story he told was of great interest to us.
Please show me the book your mum gave you.
She asked them to play with her.
We gave him an olive, but he didn't like it.
Last weekend, they went to the beach with us.

Some pronouns come *before* the verb:
I he she we they you it
Some pronouns come *after* the verb:
me him her us them you it

2 Choose the correct pronoun in the brackets.

[She Her] can ride a horse.
You can come with [I me].
[They Them] are playing chess.
Come to the park with [we us].
We had to wait for [he him].
Jack and [I me] like fishing.
[He Him] is eating ice cream.
I gave [her she] five dollars.
[I me] go to football training.
[We Us] went rockclimbing.

3 Add the missing pronouns.

Bill said to Stan, "Do ________ want to come fishing with ________?"
"Sure," Stan said and ________ went to get his fishing rod.
The boys went to the creek. ________ baited their hooks and threw their lines into the water. ________ waited and waited. At last, Stan felt something on the end of his line. "________ think I've caught a big one!" ________ shouted, pulling ________ in. Then the boys laughed. ________ was only an old brown boot.

TARGETING GRAMMAR 3 © PASCAL PRESS ISBN 9781925076592

Personal pronouns fall into three groups to represent different **persons**.

	FIRST PERSON	SECOND PERSON	THIRD PERSON
	The person speaking	**The person spoken to**	**The person/s spoken about**
Before the verb	I we	you	she he they it
After the verb	me us	you	her him them

4 Circle the pronouns. Tick which person is represented: first, second or third.

	1st	2nd	3rd
He gave her a box of chocolates.			
The horse trotted towards me, and I ran.			
You can go for a swim later.			
I am waiting for the bus.			
They took a picnic lunch with them.			

Pronouns replace nouns.

5 Here is part of a story written in third person. Write suitable pronouns in the spaces.

The screech of a parrot echoed through the valley. Suddenly, Manus froze. ________ sensed a slight movement behind him. Was ________ a possum? Or a bush turkey, perhaps? He wasn't sure. ________ crouched behind the cover of some low bushes. There was a faint sound — the sound of breathing. Manus held his breath. Fear gripped ________. The sound came closer and closer, and then ________ stopped. Leaves rustled as something moved towards ________. Would ________ be seen? ________ remained as still as a statue.

TARGETING GRAMMAR 3 © PASCAL PRESS ISBN 9781925076592

CHALLENGE

PRONOUNS

Highlight the pronouns in these texts. Are they written in the first, second or third person? Colour in your answer.

Jack waited eagerly for the new student to arrive. Andy Miggs was coming from faraway Poland and he would arrive in two days' time. He had been in touch by email, so Jack already knew quite a lot about him. He spoke good English. He was an expert skier and he was the Polish junior chess champion. But, most exciting of all, he was a whiz at computer games. There wasn't a code he couldn't crack, nor a level he couldn't reach. Jack really wanted to talk to him!

1st	2nd	3rd

"Tyson, you need to hurry! Have you packed your lunch?" Mum asked.

"Not yet, Mum," Tyson replied.

"You must hurry. The bus will be here soon. Get your books and your bag," Mum said.

"Okay. Do you know where my hat is?" Tyson asked.

1st	2nd	3rd

Dear Aunty Jane,

Last month, William and I climbed Mount Sturt. Mum probably told you all about that. We had to spend hours pulling the prickles out of our socks! Well, last Saturday, we decided to ride our horses all the way around the mountain by road. We didn't know how far it would be, nor how long it would take us, but we thought it would be good fun. Mum just rolled her eyes and said, "Watch out for snakes!"

1st	2nd	3rd

TARGETING GRAMMAR 3 © PASCAL PRESS ISBN 9781925076592

Possessive pronouns show *ownership*.
No apostrophe is needed, e.g. The red ball is **yours**, the green ball is **hers** and the blue ball is **mine**.

Singular			
mine	yours	hers	his

Plural		
ours	yours	theirs

1 Add a possessive pronoun to each sentence.

Give the book back to Ruby. It is ____________.

If this hat is ____________, come and get it.

This bike is ____________, not yours.

I found the dollar, so it is ____________.

Jack said the comic was ____________.

2 Circle the possessive pronouns. Draw an arrow to show what they 'own'.

I think this pencil is yours. He said the book was his, but it is mine.

This pencil is his, but that ruler is hers.

They paid for the ball, so it is theirs.

This blue cap is mine, not yours.

These hats are yours, but I can't see ours.

3 Write two sentences. Include the words 'mine', 'hers' and 'yours'.

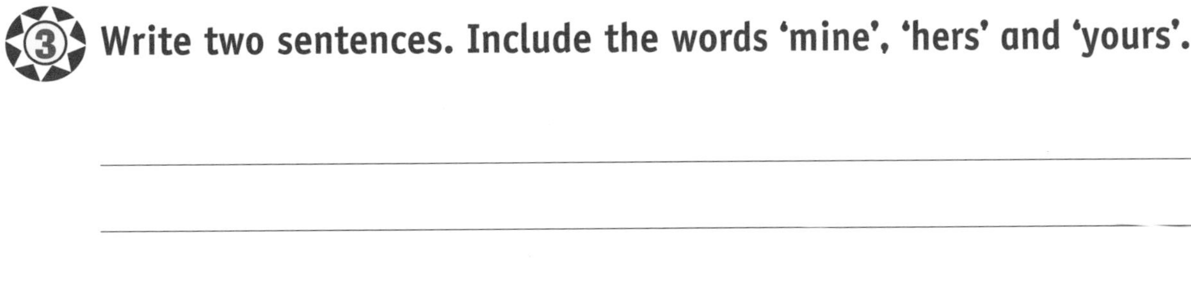

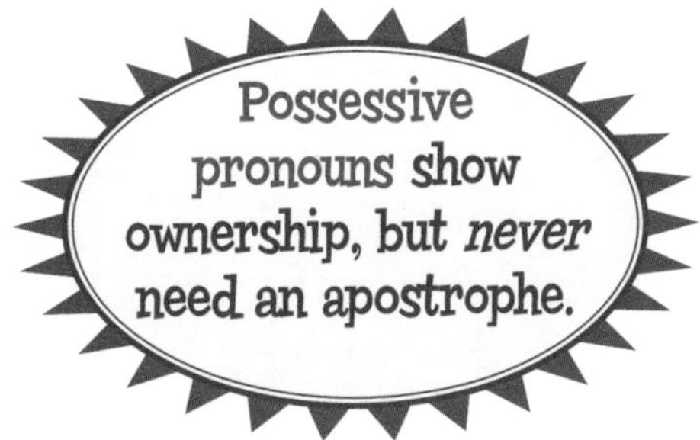

Possessive pronouns show ownership, but *never* need an apostrophe.

Pronouns usually *refer back* to a previous noun. This is called **pronoun reference**, e.g. I have a pet kitten. **She** is called Sooty. **She** likes to play with a ball and **she** likes to chase her tail.

PRONOUNS

1 The pronouns are underlined. Use an arrow to point to the nouns they refer back to.

The bucket is full of sand. It is very heavy.

Kangaroos are native animals. They live in groups called mobs.

I saw a clown on TV. He was juggling five china plates.

Sam and I like skateboarding. After school, we head for the park.

I have some pet fish. I feed them every morning.

2 Write pronouns to refer back to the nouns.

John is in a football team. ______ wears a yellow jersey.

My name is **Dana**. ______ am nine years old.

The **children** are in class. The teacher is talking to ______.

Wait here, **Jimmy**. I have a surprise for ______.

Jan saw lots of **seagulls**. ______ were flying over the fishing boats.

Pronouns can also *refer forwards* to a noun, e.g.

"May I go swimming, Mum?" **Kevin** asked. (I = Kevin)

"I've been waiting for you for ten minutes, **Lizzy**." (you = Lizzy)

3 Circle the nouns that the pronouns refer to.

"Will **you** make some pancakes?" Sammy asked his mother.

"Please, please give **me** one of your marbles," pleaded Rohan.

"Put **it** in the fridge," Jo said, handing me a bottle of softdrink.

"Have **you** read this book about dragons, Tommy?"

"Shall **we** go for a ride on our bikes?" William asked James.

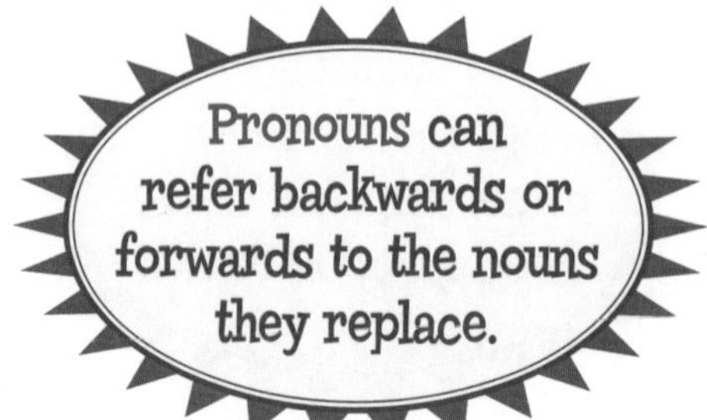

Pronouns can refer backwards or forwards to the nouns they replace.

TARGETING GRAMMAR 3 © PASCAL PRESS ISBN 9781925076592

Some **pronouns** 'mirror' their <u>subject</u>, e.g. <u>Alison</u> hurt **herself**. <u>The boys</u> helped **themselves**. These are **reflexive pronouns** and end in *self* or *selves*.

1. **Add a reflexive pronoun to each sentence.**

Liam cut ________________ with a sharp knife.

Paige has locked ________________ in her room.

I looked at ________________ in the mirror and screamed.

The children bought ________________ a lolly each.

We told ________________ to stay calm.

PRONOUNS

Questions

Some **pronouns** ask **questions**, e.g. **What** is your name? **Who** is your friend?

1. **Answer these questions.**

What is your favourite food? ________________

Who is someone you know well? ________________

Who is a person who cares for the sick? ________________

What is a person called who writes books? ________________

Who is the prime minister of Australia? ________________

2. **Add 'What' or 'Who' to ask the questions.**

________________ would you like to play?

________________ likes to sing and dance?

________________ can play chess?

________________ are you doing this weekend?

________________ do you eat for breakfast?

3. **Rewrite these questions so the words are in the correct order.**

at did zoo What see the you

____?

can the run Who fastest

____?

TARGETING GRAMMAR 3 © PASCAL PRESS ISBN 9781925076592

PRONOUNS

1 Read this short tale from Africa. Add the missing pronouns from the word box. (Some are used more than once.)

his	they	we	your	it	he	I	me	him

Anesu was a young African boy. One day, ________ went into the forest and started picking fruit. Soon, ________ heard a rustling in the bushes. There, in front of ________ , stood a terrible creature. Anesu was scared. ________ climbed a tree and began to beat ________ drum. The drumbeats said, "Help! ________ am stuck up a tree. There's a terrible creature trying to eat ________." As Anesu beat ________ drum, the creature began to dance. Finally, ________ dropped down in a deep sleep. Anesu's mum, dad and aunty arrived. ________ stood below the tree and looked up. "________ heard ________ signal for help. What's the trouble?" Anesu's dad asked.

2 Read Marisa's recount. Add the missing pronouns from the word box. (Some are used more than once.)

my	they	we	us	our	it	them	I

Hello, ________ name is Marisa. ________ live with ________ parents in Melbourne. ________ parents were born in El Salvador, a small country in Central America. ________ came to Australia when ________ was just a baby. ________ have two brothers, Lucas and Mateo. ________ like to help Mum and ________ cook tasty Salvadoran foods. *Tortillas* are ________ favourite food. ________ are like flat pancakes made from corn meal and stuffed with tasty fillings. ________ enjoy ________ very much. Another of ________ favourite foods is *arroz con leche*, a boiled rice pudding. ________ is very easy to make and is very delicious. Today, ________ are going to make *ensalada de zanahoria* (a carrot and raisin salad). ________ is a favourite with all the members of ________ family.

TARGETING GRAMMAR 3 © PASCAL PRESS ISBN 9781925076592

In any text, the **nouns** tell you who and what you are reading about: the people, the places and the things. To avoid repeating nouns, they are often *replaced* by **pronouns**. Pronouns mostly *refer back* to nouns that have already been mentioned, but they can also *refer forwards*. As you read, it is important to remember which person or thing is being talked about. Sometimes, you will need to stop and ask, "**Who** is 'she'? **Who** is 'he'? **Who** are 'they'? **What** is 'it'?" This will help you keep track of the meaning.

PRONOUNS

In this story, think about which nouns the pronouns refer to.

Terry and John spend each summer holiday on their Uncle Bill's farm. This year their uncle has a surprise for them. He has a little motorbike for each of them. The boys soon learn to ride them. One day, their uncle sets out on his bike to round up a mob of sheep. The boys are delighted when he asks them to go with him.

Draw a picture of the boys' holiday.

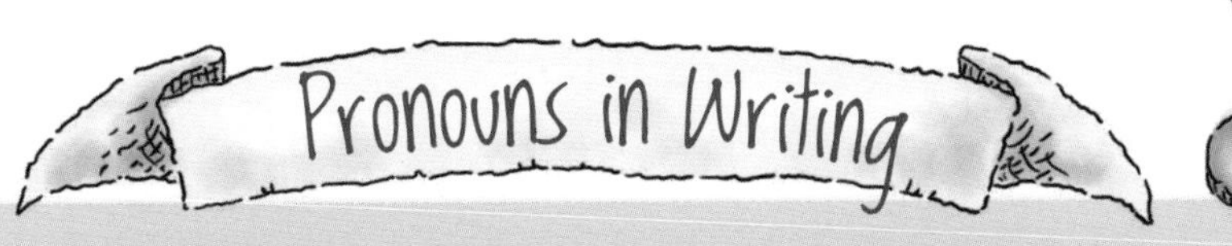

Pronouns give variety to your writing. By replacing some of the **nouns** with pronouns, your writing will flow more easily and will be more interesting to your reader.

Read this text and add the missing pronouns.

The water is rising. Antonio and Sheena are trapped by the tide in a damp, dark, sandy cave. The light from ________ torches is fading. ________ look around desperately at the steep, slimy walls. Sheena screams as something slides past ________ foot and slithers up the wall. ________ catches a glimpse of yellow eyes as ________ disappears in a flurry of green scales. Antonio looks up. ________ can see another cave high above ________. "Quickly, Sheena, ________ must hurry. The water is rising fast," ________ says.

PRONOUNS Checkpoint ☑

Circle the correct pronouns.

Mum made pancakes for [we us] to eat.

[I Me] will meet [they them] at the skate park.

[Who What] said you could go skating with [she her]?

[Her She] gave [me we] a warm blue scarf.

The boy was cold, so [he I] gave [him her] a coat.

Circle the possessive pronouns.

All of these marbles are mine.

These books are hers, not yours.

This is Jill's lunch. Tilly put hers in the bin.

Give the hat to Bob. It is his.

The pencils are ours, and the rulers are theirs.

Add a reflexive pronoun to complete each sentence.

I could do it ________________ if I tried.

Jake can climb the ladder by ________________.

Go and do it ________________!

Selena scratched ________________ on the rose bush.

They are playing in the park by ________________.

Circle ten personal pronouns in this story.

Jackson grabbed his basketball and headed for the park. There, he met his friend Mei. He asked her if she would play with him.

Mei smiled. "Yes, but I must warn you. I am pretty good!"

She was right. In their first game, she scored eight goals. Jackson only scored one. They both laughed and started the next game. Jackson was sure he would win this time.

This story is written in [1st] [2nd] [3rd] person. (Colour one.)

TARGETING GRAMMAR 3 © PASCAL PRESS ISBN 9781925076592

Write the nouns that the numbered pronouns refer to.

Dear Aunty Jane,

Last Sunday, Ben and I went bushwalking in Green Forest Park. Ben is a keen birdwatcher, so **he** (1) took his camera. **I** (2) am more interested in bugs and butterflies, so I took a net with **me** (3). Unfortunately, **we** (4) lost our way. Ben wasn't worried. **He** (5) shouted "Coo-ee" a few times and someone answered. It wasn't long before two men found us. **They** (6) showed **us** (7) the way back to the path. We followed **it** (8) back to the picnic area. **You** (9) will be pleased to know that **we** (10) won't go wandering about again without a mobile phone!

Regards,

Jacky

1	2	3	4	5
6	7	8	9	10

This recount is written in [1st] [2nd] [3rd] person. (Colour one.)

Add the missing pronouns in this story.

Henry stopped so suddenly that Harry crashed into ________.

"What's wrong?" Harry asked, rubbing ________ nose and feeling annoyed.

"I think ________ are lost," Henry breathed, looking around anxiously.

The trees stood tall and silent around ________ . The rough track ________ were following had disappeared under the damp leaves that covered the forest floor.

"Nah," said Harry. "________ can't be lost. ________ will just go back and find the track. ________ will be okay."

The boys turned and went searching for the track. ________ pushed past green ferns and dangling vines, but the track was nowhere to be found. Everything began to look the same. The trees towered over ________ like soldiers guarding ________ escape.

TARGETING GRAMMAR 3 © PASCAL PRESS ISBN 9781925076592

ADJECTIVES: Essentials

In this section, you will learn about the words that say more about **nouns**.
These 'describing' words are called **adjectives**.
Adjectives usually come before a **noun** and are part of a **noun group**.
Examples: a **green** tree, **tiny** ants, the **hot** sun, a **little** mouse, a **brick** house
By saying more about nouns, adjectives help readers 'see' what people and things look like.
Examples: I saw an animal. It was ...

a **wild** animal	a **fast** animal	a **tall** animal	a **slow** animal	a **tiny** animal

✤ TYPES OF ADJECTIVES

	Examples
Adjectives show us: • colour • number • shape • size • sound • mood	 a **red** hat, a **yellow** banana, the **blue** sky **six** eggs, **five** mice, **three** pigs a **round** table, a **square** box, an **oval** mirror a **big** truck, a **long** ribbon, a **wide** river **loud** voices, **noisy** children, a **silent** house, **happy** faces, an **angry** boy, **excited** children
Adjectives can come *before* the noun.	I saw a **large** elephant. It is a **cold, wet** day.
Adjectives can come *after* the noun.	The elephant I saw was **large**. The day is **cold** and **wet.**
Adjectives can show how two or more things *compare* with each other.	big, bigger, biggest; helpful, more helpful, most helpful
Adjectives can describe people and things in *opposite* ways. These adjectives are called **antonyms.**	hot, cold; fast, slow; happy, sad; old, new
An **adjectival phrase** is a group of words that *does the work of an adjective*. It is usually placed after the noun it describes, and is part of the **noun group**.	The boy **in striped pyjamas** A white kitten **with blue eyes** A house **on fire**

When you see this sign, you can decide whether you want to challenge yourself!

TARGETING GRAMMAR 3 © PASCAL PRESS ISBN 9781925076592

Adjectives *describe* people, places and things. They work with the noun to create a particular picture in the mind of the reader, e.g. a **tall** man; a **fat**, **sweaty** man; an **angry**, **annoyed** man.

ADJECTIVES

1 Adjectives are often part of a noun group. Circle the adjectives.

his torn clothes	the hot, bright sun	a bumbling clown
a pretty, young girl	long, dark shadows	an old wooden box
my two best friends	interesting books	a damp, dark cave

2 Write three adjectives to describe each picture.

Now use your words and pictures to write three sentences.

3 Circle the adjectives that could describe the noun in each box.

apple	sweet happy crunchy red	sky	bright blue soggy cloudy
boat	leaky cargo wooden sore	person	tasty lazy funny young
fire	smoky wet fierce cosy	ribbon	blue thin long tired

Adjectives describe **colour**, **number**, **size**, **sound** and **shape**.
Adjectives also describe **feelings** and **qualities**.

4 Place the adjectives from the box correctly in the sentences.

twelve	noisy	pink	sleepy	seven	kind	fishing	small	warm	old

There are __________ days in a week and __________ months in a year.

I heard __________ seagulls around the __________ boats.

I gave Ella two __________ boxes tied up with __________ ribbon.

The __________ boy helped the __________ lady across the street.

The __________ girl snuggled up in her __________ bed.

5 These adjectives describe a person, place or thing. Write them in the correct columns.

careless foggy sharp sandy tired overgrown
juicy polite long rocky yellow generous

PERSON	PLACE	THING
__________	__________	__________
__________	__________	__________
__________	__________	__________
__________	__________	__________

6 Circle the adjectives in this description of an imaginary creature.

PLASTIOSAURUS

This little creature is a metre in length. It has a bright green body and large brown eyes. It has a row of sharp spines along its short tail. It runs around quickly on its back legs. The Plastiosaurus likes big chunks of red meat, crunchy cockroaches and black beetles. It needs lots of exercise and a warm, cosy bed in winter.

TARGETING GRAMMAR 3 © PASCAL PRESS ISBN 9781925076592

7 Replace each number with a suitable adjective from the list.

John was in a hurry! He and his (1) __________ friends had made (2) __________ canoes, and it was the day of the (3) __________ race. He ran down to the (4) __________ shed and dragged out his own (5) __________ canoe. His (6) __________ dog, Rusty, barked at his feet.

1	many	school	best	4	tin	garden	old
2	large	dug-out	bark	5	yellow	new	painted
3	big	boat	annual	6	faithful	plump	playful

ADJECTIVES

Adjectives are often placed *after* the **noun** (or **pronoun**) they describe, e.g.
The sky is **blue**. He is **sad**. They were not **afraid**.
When two adjectives are used, they are *joined* by 'and' or 'but', e.g.
The leaves are **red** and **gold**. He was **hot** and **tired**. It is **small**, but **strong**.

8 The nouns are underlined. Highlight the adjectives.

The river is long and wide.

Sally's fat cheeks are rosy red.

Her long hair is blonde, and her eyes are green.

Bright, twinkling stars can be seen on dark nights.

After an exciting day, the climbers went home tired, but happy.

9 Add adjectives to describe the nouns in bold.

Cinderella's __________ **coach** was pulled by six __________ **horses**.

Jim was the __________ **person** to enter the __________ **shop**.

The **day** was __________ and __________, so we went to the beach.

He took a __________ **box** of __________ **books** to the library.

Dan tramped along __________ **paths** and up __________ **hills**.

Adjectives can come before or after the nouns and pronouns they describe.

ADJECTIVES

Highlight ten adjectives used in this description of a clown. Use this description to draw a picture of the clown.

The Big Top was buzzing with excitement. Clooney the clown stood waiting to enter the ring. He wore baggy pants with green and orange stripes. His coat was bright blue with pink and white spots. Around his neck, he wore a wide yellow tie.

Clooney had bushy red sideburns, and perched on top of his head was a tiny black hat. His face was chalk white, and his red lips were curved in a wide smile as if they held the laughter of the whole world. A huge red-spotted handkerchief hung from one deep pocket. Clutched in his gloved hands was a tiny green umbrella.

Clooney ran into the ring, tripping over his long, skinny shoes. He landed facedown in the sawdust to the delighted squeals of the audience.

Which adjectives might also describe Clooney in this story?

kind-hearted

old

tired

colourful

funny

angry

clumsy

magical

TARGETING GRAMMAR 3 © PASCAL PRESS ISBN 9781925076592

Participles

Participles are formed by adding **-ing** or **-ed** to the **verb**. They can be used as adjectives, e.g. an **amazing** idea, **falling** rocks, **chopped** onions, **faded** jeans, a **howling** wind.

ADJECTIVES

1 Match the adjectives (participles) to the nouns they best describe.

twinkling	baby	whipped	hen
floating	news	a speckled	singer
exciting	clouds	a puzzled	children
a sleeping	books	delighted	cream
interesting	stars	a talented	look

2 Write about ten terrified sailors on a sinking ship.

____

____

____

3 Circle the adjectives. Underline the nouns they describe.

Jessica has bought a new swimming costume.

Mosquitoes are annoying flying insects.

He carried a lighted candle into the deserted cave.

I have sliced tomatoes and grated cheese on my sandwiches.

He crossed the finishing line with a delighted shout.

4 Underline the adjectives in this story.

Jim and Perry sat beside the smoking campfire. They were warm, weary and silent now. Even the towering trees above them were drooped in sleep. Jim fell into a deep sleep, but Perry lay awake. He knew they had lost their way. How would they ever find their way out of the thick rainforest?

Participles often work as adjectives.

Punctuation stop

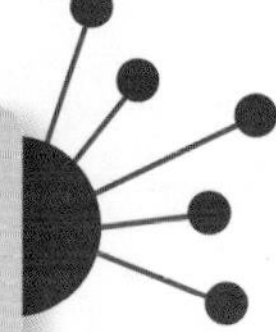

Writers mark their text to help readers make meaning.
These marks are called **punctuation marks**.

Adjectives can be joined by **'and'**, e.g. a kind **and** friendly man, a large **and** hungry lion, a sad **and** lonely boy.
OR they can be *separated* by **commas**, e.g. a kind**,** friendly man; a large**,** hungry lion; a sad**,** lonely boy.

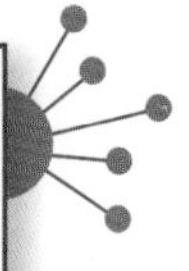

ADJECTIVES

1 Write the sentence again, using a comma in place of 'and'.

It was a long and tedious climb to the top of the hill.

____

The hot and tired and thirsty children stopped for a rest.

Only add a comma if it can replace the word 'and'!

____

Bright and colourful parrots screeched in the trees above.

____

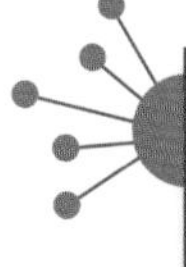

Often, the last adjective is joined by **'and'**, e.g.
He was tall, thin **and** bald. She was alone, hurt **and** desperate.

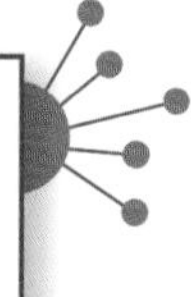

2 Mark the missing commas in this story extract.

Twenty metres below the boat, Tarquin and Sam reach the soft sandy seabed. It is scattered with small slimy rocks. They flash their torches around. Suddenly, a shadowy dark shape appears through the gloom. It is the rusting hull of an old steamship. There is a long gaping hole in its side. Tarquin leads Sam into the belly of the iron ship. They glide through dark silent cabins and drift up cracked splintered staircases ...

TARGETING GRAMMAR 3 © PASCAL PRESS ISBN 9781925076592

Adjectives can describe people and things in *opposite ways*, e.g. **happy** face, **sad** face; **new** car, **old** car; **long** rope, **short** rope. Words of opposite meaning are called **antonyms**.

Match these antonyms (opposites).

happy	young	soft	shallow
long	small	deep	low
wild	sad	heavy	fast
old	short	high	light
large	tame	slow	hard

② Write an antonym to show a contrasting idea.

Some people are **rich** and some are __________.

The bucket was __________, but now it is **empty**.

This answer is **right**, but that one is __________.

A river is __________, but a creek is **narrow**.

He washed his **dirty** clothes, so now they are __________.

Write the antonyms then search for them.

Antonyms show opposite meanings.

weak __________

awake __________

stale __________

thin __________

warm __________

new __________

smooth __________

quiet __________

F	R	E	S	H	D
A	O	Y	T	G	A
T	U	M	R	I	S
R	G	C	O	O	L
N	H	P	N	L	E
Q	W	T	G	D	E
N	O	I	S	Y	P

Adjectives can show how people or things *compare* with each other.
Add **-er** to compare *two* things.
Add **-est** to compare *more than two* things.
e.g. I have a **big** dog. Jack has a **bigger** dog. Jill has the **biggest** dog.

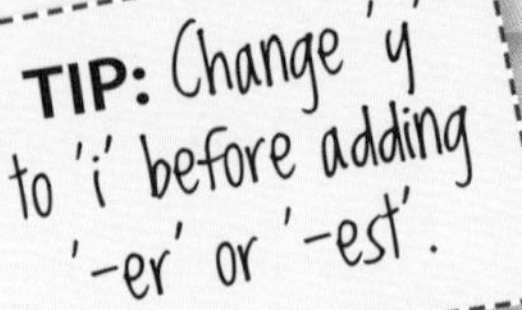

TIP: Change 'y' to 'i' before adding '-er' or '-est'.

ADJECTIVES

Complete these tables.

	Add -er	Add -est
brave		
long		
funny		
soft		
tall		

	Add -er	Add -est
short		
wild		
loud		
old		
pretty		

Circle the correct word in the brackets.

It is [hotter hottest] today than yesterday.

Jay is the [faster fastest] boy in our class.

An ostrich is [larger largest] than an emu.

January was the [wetter wettest] month this year.

Dale is the [kinder kindest] person I know.

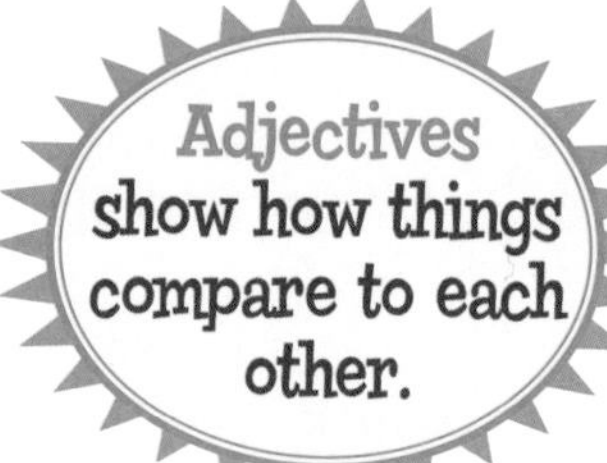

Adjectives show how things compare to each other.

Show how ideas compare with each other by adding -er or -est.

This box is big, but that one is big_____ .

Acrux is the bright_____ star in the Southern Cross.

Jess is old_____ than Kris, but young_____ than me.

The elephant is the large_____ and strong_____ land animal.

The water became deep_____ and cold_____.

Remember the spelling rules!

TARGETING GRAMMAR 3 © PASCAL PRESS ISBN 9781925076592

Nouns

page

4 Common nouns

1 Answers will vary.
2 Answers will vary.
3 castle, ship, shoes, road
4 bush, lightning, dragon, calf, monkey
5 Answers will vary.
6 emu, bird, metres, neck, feathers, legs, flowers, seeds, lizards, insects, caterpillars, female, eggs, nest, ground, chicks, grass, years

6 Common nouns: Challenge

Answers will vary.

7 Concrete and abstract nouns

1 [C]: emu, insect, rice, bucket, violin, broom, soup; [A]: love, sadness, joy, power, anger, fear, pride, beauty
2 nightfall [A], anger [A], sorrow [A], treasure [C], amazement [A]
3 excitement, freedom, embarrassment, bravery, confidence
4 Answers will vary.

8 Concrete and abstract nouns: Challenge

1 excitement, pleasure, curiosity, amazement, surprise, delight
2 Answers will vary.

9 Singular and plural nouns

1 balls, plates, foxes, brushes; koalas, peaches, games, dresses
2 boys, girls; apples, peaches, bananas; boxes, bottles; lions, tigers, ostriches; books, toys

9 Singular and plural nouns: Count and mass nouns

3 rain, coffee, snow, milk, butter, oil, cream, tea, jelly, vinegar, honey
4 children, teeth, women, geese, mice
5 babies, jockeys, countries, days, daisies
6 leaves, calves, cliffs, shelves, roofs

11 Proper nouns

1 Answers will vary.
2 Sam, Africa, Kudzi, Kudzi, Addo, Vaal River, Sam, Kudzi, Kudzi, Sam, Australia

page

3 car, Toyota; day, Thursday; subject, English; chocolate, Snickers; movie, Batman; state, Victoria; boy, Thomas
4 Answers will vary.
5 Sunday, Helen, Queensland Museum, Brisbane, Brisbane Wheel, South Bank, Brisbane, Grand Arbour, South Bank Parklands, Brisbane River, CityCat, The Spirit of Brisbane
(i) Helen, (ii) the Queensland Museum, (iii) the Brisbane Wheel, (iv) in the South Bank Parklands, (v) the Brisbane River

13 Proper nouns: Challenge

1 Sahil, India, Simran, December, Christmas Day, Bedford University, Sahil
2 It, Charles Dodgson, Lewis Carroll, Charles Dodgson, England, He, At, Oxford University, One, Liddell, Dodgson, Alice, The, Mad Hatter, Queen of Hearts, Tweedledee, Tweedledum, White Rabbit, Dodgson, The

14 Compound nouns

1 Answers will vary.
2 pathway, toothbrush, beehive; daylight, sportsground, snakebite, seatbelt
3 Answers will vary.
4 seaweed, seaside, seafood; seashore, seahorse, seagull, seabed
5 horseshoe, haystack; dragonfly, cobweb; footpath, boatshed; doughnuts, cardboard; horseback, waterfall

15 Collective nouns

1 mob, herd, swarm, flock, pod
2 pack, wolves; flock, sheep; cloud, flies; crowd, people; shoal, fish; brood, chickens; herd, elephants
3 team, stack, bunch, clump, pack

16 Collective nouns: Challenge

1 Answers will vary.
2 pack of wild dogs, brood of chicks, litter of tiny kittens, herd of cows, nest of mice

page

17 Possessive nouns: Singular

1 Sally's, dog's, teacher's, uncle's, bird's
2 friend, Jeremy, fisherman, emu, farmer
3 Answers will vary.
4 dog's, baby's, sailor's, Sue's butterfly's

18 Possessive nouns: Plural

5 dinosaurs, jockeys, students, athletes, boys
6 singular, plural, plural, singular, plural
7 The trucks are loaded with hay. A butterfly's wings are colourful. Water ran off the duck's back. A fox's tail is long and bushy.

19 Possessive nouns: Challenge

1 water's, kids', giraffe's, birds', Tim's
2 Ashar's, Tom's, farmer's, shepherd's, river's, birds', spiders', fox's, turtles', duck's
3 the boy's hat, a baby's rattle, Jessie's balloon, birds' feathers, dogs' bones, a girl's bike, a man's shoe, Katy's bear, Tommy's ball

20 Nouns: Punctuation stop

1 One of Australia's best-known bush poets is 'Banjo' Paterson. He was born more than 150 years ago and grew up in country New South Wales. He went to a school in Sydney and later worked at a law firm.
One of his best-known poems is *The Man from Snowy River*. He also wrote the words of the famous song *Waltzing Matilda*. His face appears on the Australian $10 note.
2 Oranges, lemons and limes are all citrus fruits. The farmer keeps horses, cows, pigs, ducks and hens. Wheat, sugar, coal and iron ore are exported to Asia. Dairy products include milk, cheese, butter and yoghurt. Jill's three best friends are Sue, Judy and Carol.
3 dad's, giraffe's, students', sister's, sharks'
4 have not, haven't; was not, wasn't; could not, couldn't; has not, hasn't; he is, he's; you are, you're; we had, we'd; I am, I'm; they have, they've
5 isn't, We've, weren't, It's, won't, couldn't

22 Noun groups

1 Answers will vary.

page

2 (images clockwise from top right) a basket of fruit; a can of orange paint; a clown with a red nose; tiny black ants; a fox with a bushy tail; the long, thin snake
3 Answers will vary.
4 Answers will vary.

23 Noun groups: Determiners

5 his, a, its, each; their, every, some, my; the, her, these, that
6 <u>that steep</u> **mountain**; **the boys** <u>in my class</u>; <u>My two best</u> **friends**; <u>some sweet and creamy chocolate</u> **puddings**; <u>Dark, grey</u> **thunderclouds**; <u>Those three black</u> **horses** <u>in the stable</u>
7 an, a/the; the, the, the; an, an; the, the, the; an, a; the, the
8 (images clockwise from top right) a spider's web; Molly's ballet slippers; birds' feathers; a carpenter's tool; a chef's hat; riders' helmets; a man's red tie; the boy's kite

24 Noun groups: Joining word 'and'

9 the lions, tigers and camels; Jess and William/the museum and the art gallery; the captain and his men/a long and dusty road; emails and text messages/my mobile phone; Tennis, hockey and basketball/my favourite sports

25 Noun groups: Challenge

Answers will vary.
Noun group examples: a round platform, some horses made of wood, bright colours, a saddle and a bridle, a wooden post.
Caption examples: A carousel is a ride for young children. A carousel is a merry-go-round.

26 Nouns in reading

A huge wave; the sea; the little sailing boat; a leaf in the wind; The mast; the boat; the swirling water; The wave; the helpless boat; the sharp rocks; The wave; The boat; pieces, scattered across the sand like matchsticks

26 Nouns in writing

Answers will vary.

27 Nouns: Checkpoint

1 clouds, top, cheek, Things, sky, snowflakes, mountain, air, clouds, sun

page

2 Anzac Day, Australian, Gallipoli, World War, Australians, Australian War Memorial, Canberra
3 happiness (A), parrot (C), curiosity (A), pride (A), library (C)
4 sportsground, sunshine, sunlight, lighthouse, toothbrush, seatbelt
5 Count nouns: avocado, potato, storm, flower, cloud
Mass nouns: water, sand, wheat, oil, cream
6 Pietro leads his donkey down the narrow mountain path to the fishing village of Mondova. He has baskets of olives and nuts, yellow cheeses, jars of olive oil, and crab pots woven by his father. He enters the crowded marketplace and finds his grandfather. He is already busy selling salted fish, grapes, juicy oranges and flat rounds of bread.
7 Last Saturday, it was Tom's ninth birthday. He shouted with delight when he saw his dad's present. It was a little black and white puppy. His mum gave him a shiny red skateboard. When he opened his gran's present, he found a book, a game, a toy truck and a box of chocolates. Tom said a happy thank you to all his family.

PRONOUNS

30 Personal pronouns: Singular and plural
1 he, us; me, you; she, them, her; we, him, he, it; they, us
2 She, me, They, us, him; I, He, her, I, We
3 you, me, he, They, They, I, he, it, It

31 Personal pronouns: Person
4 He, her (3rd); me, I (1st); You (2nd); I (1st); They, them (3rd)
5 He, it, He, him, it, him, he, He

32 Personal pronouns: Challenge
1 3rd
2 2nd
3 1st

33 Possessive pronouns
1 hers; yours; theirs/mine/hers/his/ours; mine; yours/his/theirs

page

2 yours (pencil), his (book), mine (book); his (pencil), hers (ruler); theirs (ball); mine (cap), yours (cap); yours (hats), ours (hats)
3 Answers will vary.

34 Pronoun reference
1 bucket, Kangaroos, clown, Sam and I, fish
2 He, I, them, you, They
3 mother, Rohan, bottle (of softdrink), Tommy, William (and) James

35 Reflexive pronouns
1 himself, herself, myself, themselves, ourselves

35 Questions
1 Answers will vary.
2 What, Who, Who, What, What
3 What did you see at the zoo? Who can run the fastest?

36 Pronouns: Challenge
1 he, he, him, He, his, I, me, his, it, They, We, your
2 my, I, my, My, They/We, I, I, They, me, our/my, They, We/I, them, our/my, It, we, It, our

37 Pronouns in reading

Terry and John spend each summer holiday on **their** (Terry and John) Uncle Bill's farm. This year **their** (Terry and John) uncle has a surprise for **them**. (Terry and John) **He** (Uncle Bill) has a little motorbike for each of **them**. (Terry and John) The boys soon learn to ride **them**. (the motorbikes) One day, **their** (Terry and John) uncle sets out on **his** (Uncle Bill) bike to round up a mob of sheep. The boys are delighted when **he** (Uncle Bill) asks **them** (Terry and John) to go with **him**. (Uncle Bill)

37 Pronouns in writing

their, They, her, She, it, He, them, we, he

38 Pronouns: Checkpoint
1 us; I, them; Who, her; She, me; I, him
2 mine; hers, yours; hers; his; ours, theirs
3 myself, himself, yourself, herself, themselves
4 his, he, his, He, her, she, him, I, you, I, She, their, she, They, he

This story is written in 3rd person.

page

5 1 Ben; 2 Jacky; 3 Jacky; 4 Ben, Jacky; 5 Ben; 6 two men; 7 Ben, Jacky; 8 the path; 9 Aunty Jane; 10 Ben, Jacky

This recount is written in 1st person.

6 him, his, we, them, they, We, We, We, They, them, their

ADJECTIVES

41 Adjectives

1 torn; hot, bright; bumbling; pretty, young; long, dark; old, wooden; two, best; interesting; damp, dark
2 Answers will vary.
3 apple: sweet, crunchy, red; boat: leaky, wooden, cargo; fire: smoky, fierce, cosy; sky: bright, blue, cloudy; person: lazy, funny, young; ribbon: blue, thin, long
4 seven, twelve; noisy, fishing; small, pink; kind, old; sleepy, warm
5 Person: careless, tired, polite, generous
Place: foggy, sandy, overgrown, rocky
Thing: sharp, juicy, long, yellow
6 little, bright, green, large, brown, sharp, short, back, big, red, crunchy, black, warm, cosy
7 Answers will vary.
8 long, wide (river); fat, rosy, red (cheeks); long, blonde (hair), green (eyes); bright, twinkling (stars), dark (nights); exciting (day), tired, happy (climbers)
9 Answers will vary.

44 Adjectives: Challenge

baggy, green, orange, bright, blue, pink, white, wide, yellow, bushy, red, tiny, black, chalk, white, red, wide, whole, huge, red-spotted, one, deep, gloved, tiny, green, long, skinny, delighted

45 Participles

1 floating clouds, exciting news, a sleeping baby, interesting books; whipped cream, a speckled hen, a puzzled look, delighted children, a talented singer
2 Answers will vary.
3 **Adjective**, noun: **new swimming** costume; **annoying flying** insects; **lighted** candle, **deserted** cave; **sliced** tomatoes, **grated** cheese; **finishing** line, **delighted** shout
4 smoking, warm, weary, silent, towering, deep, thick

page

46 Adjectives: Punctuation stop

1 It was a long, tedious climb to the top of the hill.
The hot, tired, thirsty children stopped for a rest.
Bright, colourful parrots screeched in the trees above.
2 soft, sandy seabed; small, slimy rocks; shadowy, dark shape; long, gaping hole; dark, silent cabins; long, broken staircases

47 Antonyms

1 long, short; wild, tame; old, young; large, small; soft, hard; deep, shallow; heavy, light; high, low; slow, fast
2 poor, full, wrong, wide, clean
3 weak, strong; awake, asleep; stale, fresh; thin, fat; warm, cool; new, old; smooth, rough; quiet, noisy

F	R	E	S	H	D
A	O	Y	T	G	A
T	U	M	R	I	S
R	G	C	O	O	L
N	H	P	N	L	E
Q	W	T	G	D	E
N	O	I	S	Y	P

48 Comparing

1 braver, bravest; longer, longest; funnier, funniest; softer, softest; taller, tallest; shorter, shortest; wilder, wildest; louder, loudest; older, oldest; prettier, prettiest
2 hotter, fastest, larger, wettest, kindest
3 bigger; brightest; older, younger; largest, strongest; deeper, colder

49 Comparing: 'Best'/'Worst'

4 best; better; better; good
5 bad; worst; bad, worse; worst

49 Comparing: 'More'/'Less'

6 most; more; most; more
7 least; less; least; less

50 Prepositional phrases

1 Answers will vary.
2 in/with, of, with, above, by/under/near/beside, without/with, on, under/beside
3 with, on/down/along/across, of, in, of, for, on, with

51 Adjectival phrases

1 **man** with a long beard; **box** of fish

TARGETING GRAMMAR 3 © PASCAL PRESS ISBN 9781925076592

page

sinkers; **chocolate** in the gold wrapper; **nest** in the tree; **dog** with long, shaggy ears
2 The box of books is heavy. A girl with blue eyes got on the bus. He gave his mum six roses with long stems.
3 Answers will vary.

52 Adjectives in reading

snooty, rich, pink, fairy, pink, pink, beautiful, black, fancy, pink, gorgeous, lovely, cherry, red, wide, toothy, bright, pink

52 Adjectives in writing

Answers will vary.

53 Adjectives: Checkpoint

1 angry, thick, blood-red, Brilliant, ash-dark, Hot, fiery, little, fishing, churning, blue, red, empty, awful, stinging, burning
2 Answers will vary.
3 Answers will vary.
4 sweet, sour; ugly, beautiful; easy, hard; front, back; wrong, right; same, different; loud, quiet; strong, weak; huge, tiny; simple, difficult
5 more, highest, faster, least, better, worse
6 **A** cold**,** icy wind moaned around **W**illiam's small tent**.**
She has a skipping rope with shiny**,** glittering handles**.**
The man was tall and powerful with a short**,** pointed beard**.**
Captain **W**ong heard the loud**,** droning noise of a helicopter**.**
The basket was full of sweet**,** juicy**,** delicious apples**.**

Verbs

56 'Doing' verbs

1 People, **verbs:** Dennis **waited**, farmer **plants**, Mum **cooks**, Cinderella **lost**, ballerina **twirled**
2 Answers will vary.
3 bounced; kicked, scored; throw, catch; bucked, fell; rang, ran, answered

57 Commands

1 Write; Draw; Wash; Put; Meet
2 Sit, eat; Clean, go; Feed, take; Come, play; Close, open

page

3 Do not wait for me. (Don't wait for me.); Do not throw the ball back. (Don't throw the ball back.); Do not shut the door. (Don't shut the door.); Do not open the window. (Don't open the window.)

58 'Saying' verbs

1 asked, laughed, whispered, screamed, cried
2 roosters crow, mice squeak, elephants trumpet; wolves howl, monkeys chatter, frogs croak, horses neigh
3 Answers will vary.
4 Answers will vary.

59 Verbs: Punctuation stop

"Dinner is ready**,"** Mum called.
"Who would like a pizza**?"** asked Dad.
Paul said**, "**I think it will rain this afternoon.**"**
"I never get all my sums right**,"** Zara grumbled.
Eddie said**, "**I'm playing cricket on Saturday.**"**

60 Subject

1 The Smith twins; Our class; They; Wild geese; The pipe band
2 Five little chicks hatched from the eggs. Some of the students play violins. The tennis ball bounced high over the net. The wind blew the dark clouds away. Mr Adams grows cucumbers in his garden.
3 Answers will vary.

61 Subject-verb agreement

1 go, runs, drives, drink, wishes
2 swims, swim; are, is; rides, ride; like, likes; cries, cry
3 Answers will vary.

62 Subject: Challenge

Puppets, They, The puppeteer; People, They; *Finger puppets*, You; *Glove puppets*, You; *Rod puppets*, Chinese festival dragons, They; *Shadow puppets*, The puppeteer, The people; *Marionettes (marry-on-nets)*, Strings, The puppeteer, One of the most famous puppet plays, It

63 Object

1 the clothes; an interesting book; sausages; my ball, it; the baseball game
2 Object: Mr Free bakes bread, pies and pastries. The chef threw the scraps in the bin. Benson scored five goals in the first half of the game.
3 Answers will vary.

page

64 Commands (Subject/object)

1 your schoolbooks; the dog; your sister; your poem; the ball, it

2 a slice of bread; mustard; a slice of ham and a slice of cheese; another slice of bread; some butter; the sandwich; the sandwich; your snack

3 Answers will vary.

65 Linking verbs

1 is; is; am; are; is, is

2 was, was, were, was, Were

3 be, been, being, been, be

66 Verb groups

1 is riding; can jump; has fallen; are skating; will finish, will go

2 <u>Subject</u>, **verb**; <u>The soldiers</u> **were marching**; <u>Jane</u> **can swim**; <u>The two boys</u> **have been sliding**; <u>We</u> **are waiting**; <u>The men</u> **have been fishing**

3 Answers will vary.

67 Verbs: Challenge

1 was shining; was catching; were sitting; were watching; were bringing; were talking, eating and drinking; were sitting; were drinking; have been carrying

2 was, were, was, was, was

68 Verb tenses

1 Past, Future, Present, Past, Past

2 I try, you try, it tries; I sneeze, you sneeze, he sneezes; I wish, you wish, she wishes; I hurry, you hurry, he hurries

3 played, cried, rolled; trotted, hurried, cooked, stopped

4 will meet, will go, will fly, will (you) play

69 Helping (auxiliary) verbs

1 is playing; are watching; am training; is walking, is riding; are collecting; I am going

2 were collecting, was floating, was conducting, were waiting, was reading, were gathering

70 'Have' verbs

1 have, had, have, having, have

2 has, have, having, had, has

3 has/had planted, Have (you) finished, has/had painted, Has (Nathan) mowed, have/had (never) played

page

71 Regular verbs

1 performing; lifted, cooking; likes/liked; wanted; watches; hurrying

71 Irregular verbs

1 slid, broke, ate, wrote, drove

2 ran, stood, know, took, fly

72 Modal (auxiliary) verbs

1 can, will, could, must/should, may/might

2 wouldn't, mustn't, couldn't, won't, shouldn't

3 Can, May/Can/Should, Will, Could/Would/Will, Would

73 Verbs in reading

Answers will vary.

73 Verbs in writing

Answers will vary.

74 Verbs: Checkpoint

1 **Action verb**, <u>saying verb</u>: Suddenly, there is a noise like a big wind and the ground **shakes** violently.
"Quick, **run**! The volcano is about to blow!" <u>shouts</u> Benson. Bee and Benson **run** across the crater floor and over the rim. They **slither** down the mountainside. Behind them, the volcano **explodes**, sending ash high into the air.
"Faster!" <u>yells</u> Bee, as rocks **rain** down on them and a river of hot lava **spills** from the crater. They **stumble** to the helicopter. Benson **starts** the engine, and the blades **spin** round and round. They **lift** to safety, just as the red fingers of hot lava **reach** the landing skids.

2 <u>Subject</u>, **verb**: <u>The pirates</u> **hid**; <u>the divers</u> **discovered**; <u>Freshwater crocodiles</u> **eat**; <u>The farmers</u> **have been harvesting**; <u>Oranges, lemons and mandarins</u> **are**

3 two eggs, your name, a bucket, two pieces of fruit, your homework

4 **"**You are late again,**"** says the teacher, glaring at Sam.
"Sorry, Miss Tibbs,**"** mumbles Sam.
"What's the reason this time**?"** she asks him with a sigh.
"I missed the bus,**"** Sam mutters.
"That's three times this week, Sam,**"** Miss Tibbs grumbles.

5 are, Have, did, been, were

6 Future, Past, Present, Future, Past

7 floated, bit, blew, hid, rested

8 would, Will/Would/Can, can, must, might

TARGETING GRAMMAR 3 © PASCAL PRESS ISBN 9781925076592

Adverbs

page

77 Adverbs

1 fast; loudly, angrily; hard; well; quickly, carefully
2 always, sometimes, forever, later, soon
3 somewhere; away; here, there; anywhere; backwards, forwards
4 regularly, Yesterday, well, soon, behind, forward, easily, triumphantly

78 Adverbs of manner

1 brightly, lazily, locally, carefully; easily, secretly, gently, helpfully
2 lazily; brightly, gently; carefully; easily; locally
3 angrily, heavily, neatly, eagerly

79 Questions

1 Where, When, How, Why
2 Answers will vary.
3 How, Where, Why, Where, When

80 Prepositional phrases

1 Answers will vary.
2 with; on/along/across; during; beside/behind/with; in/near/beside/around/behind; before/after; across; beneath/below/under
3 from, between, of, by/from, of, of

81 Adverbial phrases

1 When, Why; How, Where; Where, When; Where, Why; Where, When
2 in ten minutes, with a soft cloth, below the waves, for his bravery, During the storm
3 Answers will vary.

82 Adverbs: Challenge

to them, back to help you, bravely, into his pocket, on the back of the photo, to Mangivar, back to the army camp, to the captain

83 Adverbs in reading

Answers will vary.

83 Adverbs in writing

Answers will vary.

84 Adverbs: Checkpoint

1 along the beach, merrily in the wind, playfully at their heels, onto the rocks, high into the air, there like a rainbow
2 in; on/with; behind; down/along/across; against, of

page

3 On warm, summer days (when), in the pool (where); At the toy shop (where), for me (why); In the morning (when), to the beach (where) for a holiday (why)
4 Where, When, How, Why

Sentences

86 Sentences: Statements

1 Answers will vary.
2 **G**old is easy to shape because it is soft**.** **I**t can be beaten into paper-thin sheets or stretched into fine wire**.** **G**old will only melt at very high temperatures**.** **I**t will not rust or tarnish**.** **T**hese qualities make it a long-lasting metal of great beauty**.**

Every day at sunset, a pesky fox comes prowling around the henhouse disturbing our chooks**.** **T**he chooks cluck and cackle and scramble back to the safety of their perches**.** **T**here are feathers everywhere, and the chooks have gone off laying eggs**.** **D**ad says something has to be done**.**

87 Subject

1 This shy and unusual animal; A man on a motorbike; we; Peaches, plums and apricots; a basket of bread.

87 Subject: Subject-verb agreement

2 were, have, closes, has, is
3 Subject, **verb**: Jackson and his two friends **are riding**; She **has been swimming**; The men in the boxing ring **are wearing**; Several of the fishermen **caught**; leaves and branches **littered**

88 Object

1 fairy floss; a packet of potato chips; the hot, sandy desert; your shoes; a chocolate cake with pink icing
2 Elephants have a long trunk and long ivory tusks.
Dan will buy oranges, apples and bananas.
Mum heated the custard in the microwave.

TARGETING GRAMMAR 3 © PASCAL PRESS ISBN 9781925076592

page

3 The angry giant (subject) snapped (verb) the branch (object) with his bare hands. Each of the kids in my class (subject) made (verb) an animal (object) out of clay.
Jack and Jill (subject) took (verb) the pail of water (object) to the bottom of the hill.
We (subject) rode (verb) our horses (object) along the grassy hills above the city.
The man in the yellow life jacket (subject) paddled (verb) his kayak (object) down the river.

89 Building statements

Answers will vary.

90 Commands

1 read; Open, empty; Put, don't touch; Whip, add; swim
2 **Verb**, object: **Snap** your fingers and **click** your heels. **Boil** the potatoes in a saucepan. Please **handle** this old vase with great care.

90 Exclamations

1 Answers will vary.

91 Questions

1 When, How, Why/How; Who, Which, What
2 Will Dan go to the beach today? Have you seen this movie before? Would they like pancakes and syrup? Can we go for a swim in the pool later?
3 don't you? will you? do they? can't you? is he?

92 Compound sentences

1 and, so/and, or, and, but, or
2 but, and, and, or, so, but
3 There's room in our car **so** you can come with us. I eat lettuce **but** I don't like cucumber. It rained heavily last night **so** the tanks are full. Ken would like to come **but** his dad won't let him. Zeb saved his money **so** he could buy a model plane.

page

93 Subject: Challenge

1 **Subject**, joining word: **They** waited for twenty minutes, but **the bus** didn't come. (different); **Dad** lifted me onto his shoulders, so **I** could see the parade. (different); **I** would like to make pancakes, but **I** don't know how. (same); **You** must hurry, or **you** will miss the bus. (same); **Sally** will wash the dishes, and **Bo** will dry them. (different)
2 We, it (D); Maree, she (S); Josh, his team (D); You, you (S); I, the potatoes (D); Terry, it (D); Gus, he (S); Tess, Tina (D)

94 Sentences in reading

Answers will vary.

94 Sentences in writing

Answers will vary.

95 Sentences: Checkpoint

1 Answers will vary.
2 Many tourists, Cricket balls and cricket bats, our team, Jason, A girl wearing a hat and sunglasses
3 the jelly; all the doors and windows; your ball; the cards, them; your name and address
4 go, are, have, plays, done
5 but, and, but, so, or
6 **O**ranges**,** lemons and limes are citrus fruits grown in **A**ustralia**. G**rapefruit**,** mandarins and cumquats are also citrus fruits**. C**itrus fruits have orange**,** yellow or green skins**. T**he soft pulp inside is divided into sections**. M**ost citrus fruits contain seeds**.**
Most of Australia**'**s citrus crops are oranges**. A** large part of each year**'**s crop goes into the making of juice**. S**ome oranges are made into a jam called marmalade**.**
7 Answers will vary.

TARGETING GRAMMAR 3 © PASCAL PRESS ISBN 9781925076592

Some adjectives compare things in a *special way*.

good **better** **best**

bad **worse** **worst**

4 Choose the correct word from 'good', 'better' or 'best'.

She is the ______________ friend I have ever had.

Jack is a ______________ speller than I am.

My maths is good, but it could be ______________.

Everyone had a ______________ time at my birthday party.

5 Choose the correct word from 'bad', 'worse' or 'worst'.

One apple in the dish has gone ______________.

It was the ______________ storm in five years.

I had a __________ cold, but now it is ______________.

That was the ______________ game the Reds have played all season.

'More' / 'Less'

To compare adjectives that have *more than one syllable*, use **'more'** and **'most'**, or **'less'** and **'least'**.

useful **more** useful **most** useful

useful **less** useful **least** useful

Exception: words ending in **'y'** (busy busier busiest)

6 Correctly add 'more' or 'most' to these sentences.

Who is the ______________ famous person you know?

I don't know which is ______________ delicious, ice cream or custard.

We have had a ______________ exciting day.

Please be ______________ careful with your spelling.

Some comparing adjectives have special forms.

7 Correctly add 'less' or 'least' to these sentences.

That sum was the ______________ difficult I've done.

At our school, hockey is ______________ popular than soccer.

Aden was the ______________ adventurous boy in the group.

As the kitten grew, she became ______________ playful.

ADJECTIVES

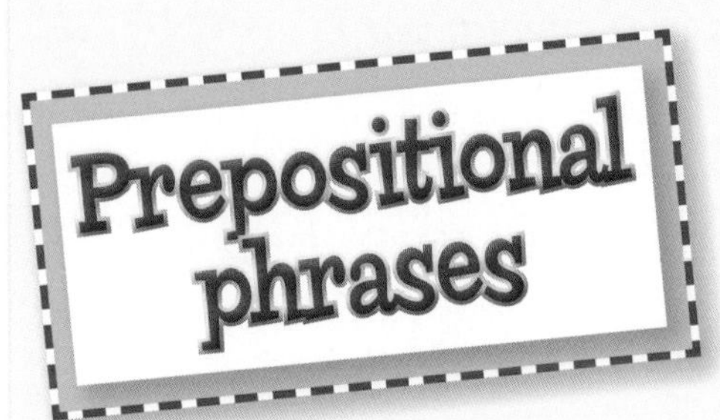

A **phrase** is a group of words *without* a **verb**. It is often introduced by a **preposition** and is called a **prepositional phrase**.

A **prepositional phrase** does the work of an:

(i) adjective (adjectival phrase) *The girl **in a pink dress**.*

(ii) adverb (adverbial phrase) *He ran **across the sand**.*

ADJECTIVES

1 Write some prepositional phrases.

____

____

____

____

____

____

____

____

about	*behind*	*from*	*through*
above	*below*	*in*	*till*
across	*beneath*	*into*	*to*
after	*beside*	*near*	*towards*
against	*between*	*of*	*under*
along	*by*	*off*	*until*
almost	*down*	*on*	*up*
around	*during*	*over*	*upon*
at	*except*	*past*	*with*
before	*for*	*since*	*without*

2 Choose a preposition to complete each adjectival phrase.

Prepositional phrases can do the work of adjectives.

The boy __________ striped pyjamas has a teddy bear.

She picked a bunch __________ red roses.

I have blue socks __________ white stripes.

He couldn't reach the shelf __________ his head.

The seat __________ the window is mine.

Who is that boy __________ a hat?

The clock __________ the wall has stopped.

The slippers __________ the bed are my mother's.

3 Add the missing prepositions.

My dad is a painter. He has a red ute __________ his name written __________ the side. The other day, I carried his box __________ tools to his ute and put it ______ the back. I helped him load his cans ______ paint and some rags __________ cleaning up any spills. Finally, we put a ladder ______ top. Dad tied everything down __________ a strong rope.

TARGETING GRAMMAR 3 © PASCAL PRESS ISBN 9781925076592

Adjectival phrases

An **adjectival phrase** is usually placed *after* the noun it describes and is part of the **noun group**. Adjectival phrases answer *which* about the noun, e.g. a boy **in a blue shirt**, the books **on the table**, a vase **of flowers**.

1 Underline the adjectival phrases that describe the nouns.

On the stairs, I met a **man** with a long beard.

Dad bought another **box** of fish sinkers.

Sam chose the **chocolate** in the gold wrapper.

The **nest** in the tree belongs to a currawong.

Jeremy bought a **dog** with long, shaggy ears.

An adjectival phrase often begins with a preposition.

An **adjectival phrase** is always placed *close* to the **noun** it describes.

☑ The boy in blue jeans ate the apple.

☒ The boy ate the apple in blue jeans.

2 Unscramble these sentences.

books heavy **box** is the of

____

bus eyes got the **girl** a blue on with

____

his stems he long **roses** gave with mum six

____

3 Add an adjectival phrase to describe the noun in the noun group.

The old man ________________________ gave me a dollar.

I have a bike ________________________.

A shark ________________________ glided through the water.

In any text, the **nouns** tell you *who* and *what* you are reading about: the people, places and things. Writers use **adjectives** to give *more information* about nouns, so that readers can better imagine them and understand their actions. Writers influence their readers by choosing their adjectives carefully. For example, readers understand who the 'goodies' and the 'baddies' are by the way the author describes them.

ADJECTIVES

Circle the adjectives in this description of Mary-Jane Austen, then draw a picture of what you imagine she looks like.

Anyone could see that Mary-Jane Austen was one of those snooty rich girls. She was wearing a dress like pink fairy floss. She had pink bows on her dress and pink bows in her beautiful black hair. She even had fancy pink thongs on her feet. Yep! MJ was gorgeous. She turned her lovely face towards me. Her cherry red lips parted in a wide toothy smile. It was like a burst of sunshine. I felt my knees wobble and my face turned bright pink.

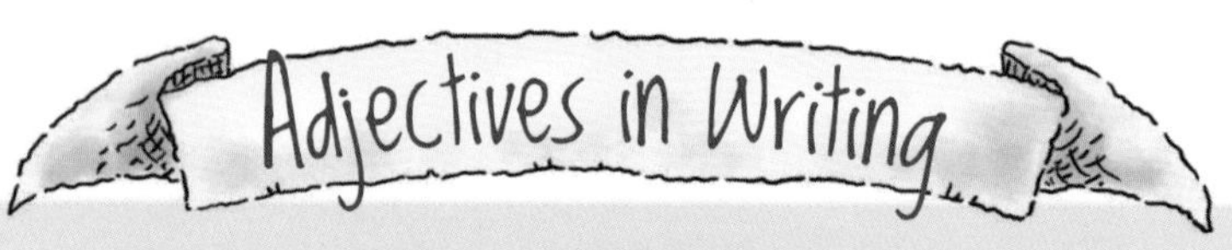

When you are writing a text, use **adjectives** (and adjectival phrases) with your nouns to show your reader what the people, places and things look like. You can paint great pictures by using great adjectives!

Create an imaginary creature that roams the desert in search of food. In your notebook, write a short and colourful paragraph to show your reader exactly what it looks like. When you have finished, ask a friend to read your description and draw a picture of your creature.

A capital letter begins a sentence.

A full stop ends a sentence.

Commas separate words in a list.

TARGETING GRAMMAR 3 © PASCAL PRESS ISBN 9781925076592

ADJECTIVES Checkpoint ☑

Circle ten different adjectives in this extract from *The Treasures of D'Arcora*.

Pietro looks up at the angry mountain. The thick cloud above it glows blood-red. Brilliant flashes of lightning split the ash-dark sky. Hot, fiery rocks burst from the top and shower down over the little fishing village. They sizzle and steam as they splash into the churning blue waters of the bay. Rivers of red lava spill down the empty streets of Mandova. An awful smell fills the air, stinging eyes and burning noses.

Add adjectives and/or adjectival phrases to expand these noun groups.

a dog ____________________

the flowers ____________________

a dolphin ____________________

the moon ____________________

a mountain ____________________

Illustrate these noun groups.

a tall ship with large white sails	a chocolate cake on a round plate	a red flag flapping in the wind

TARGETING GRAMMAR 3 © PASCAL PRESS ISBN 9781925076592

Join the antonyms.

sweet	hard	same	difficult
ugly	back	loud	tiny
easy	sour	strong	quiet
front	right	huge	different
wrong	beautiful	simple	weak

Choose the correct word in the brackets.

Some snakes are [more most] venomous than others.

Mount Everest is the [higher highest] mountain in the world.

A tiger is [faster fastest] than a lion.

Red is the [less least] common hair colour.

Toby is a [good better] batsman than I am.

My score on the test was [worse worst] than before.

Punctuate the sentences.

a cold icy wind moaned around williams small tent

she has a skipping rope with shiny glittering handles

the man was tall and powerful with a short pointed beard

captain wong heard the loud droning noise of a helicopter

the basket was full of sweet juicy delicious apples

TARGETING GRAMMAR 3 © PASCAL PRESS ISBN 9781925076592

VERBS: Essentials

In this section, you will learn about the words that say what is 'happening' in a sentence. These 'happening' words are called **verbs**. They tell us what people are doing, thinking, saying and feeling.

The job of some verbs is just to *hold two ideas* together.
Examples: The box **is** heavy. The children **are** friends.

The verb is the heart of a sentence.

✤ TYPES OF VERBS	*Examples*
'Doing' (action) verbs express what people and things are *doing*. A **command** begins with a doing verb.	walk, eat, ride, cry, smell, swim, read
'Saying' verbs show *how* people (and animals) *express* their feelings.	shout, whisper, say, speak, roar, bark, growl
Linking verbs (is, are, was, were) do not express action. They *connect ideas* about the subject, by describing it or renaming it.	The moon **is** yellow. The girls **are** dancers. He **was** late. They **were** tired.
The Big Four (is, are, was, were) are often part of a **verb group**. They show *when* things are happening: NOW or in the PAST. The words they help often end in **-ing.**	NOW: Tony **is walking** to school. The boys **are playing** cricket. PAST: Jan **was eating** her lunch. The children **were reading** books.
Helping verbs *help* other verbs and participles in a verb group.	I **have been waiting** for you. We **will go** home. John **has done** his work.
Modal verbs are special helping verbs that express *obligation*, *intention* and *possibility*.	She **can swim**. You **must wait** for me. I **might go** to the movies.

✤ PARTICIPLES	*Examples*
Present participle = verb + -ing	go → **going**
Past participle (regular) = verb + -ed (or -en)	cook → cook**ed**, eat → eat**en**

✤ VERBS IN SENTENCES

Every sentence must have a verb.	*Examples*
The verb can be *one word*.	The dog **ran** away. The girl **is** happy.
The verb can be *more than one* word. This is a **verb group.** It is made up of a **helping verb/s** (auxiliary verb) and a **participle.**	The man **is climbing** a ladder. He **has been waiting** for me. The moon **was hidden** by clouds.
Every sentence has a **subject.** It is a **noun group** or **pronoun.** This is the part that tells you *who* or *what* the sentence is about.	**Lara** walks to school. **The boys** ride bikes. **My sister and brother** are in high school.
Action verbs are often followed by an **object**. An **object** *receives the action* of the subject.	The dog (subject) ate (*doing verb*) the bone (**object**). Bob *likes* **pizza.** I *eat* **pies.**

Subject-verb agreement

A **subject** and a **verb** must *agree* in **number.**	*Examples*
A **singular verb** is used with a **singular** subject.	An owl **hunts** at night. A cow **eats** grass.
A **plural verb** is used with a **plural** subject.	Owls **hunt** at night. Cows **eat** grass.

✤ VERB TENSE

Verbs show when events take place: NOW in the present, in the PAST and in the FUTURE.	*Examples*
NOW (*present tense*)	Mike **plays** cricket. Mike **is playing** cricket.
PAST (*past tense*)	Sam **played** cricket. Sam **was playing** cricket.
TOMORROW (*future tense*)	They **will play** the final cricket match on Saturday.

When you see this sign, you can decide whether you want to challenge yourself!

'Doing' verbs

'Doing' verbs are verbs of *action*. They tell you what people and things *do*, e.g. Birds **fly**. Bells **ring**. Rain **falls**. Fires **burn**. Children **play**. Fish **swim**.

1

Underline the people. Circle the verbs that say what they are doing.

Dennis waited patiently for the school bus.

Each year, the farmer plants a crop of wheat.

Mum cooks bacon and eggs for breakfast.

Cinderella lost her glass slipper on the stairs.

The ballerina twirled on the tips of her toes.

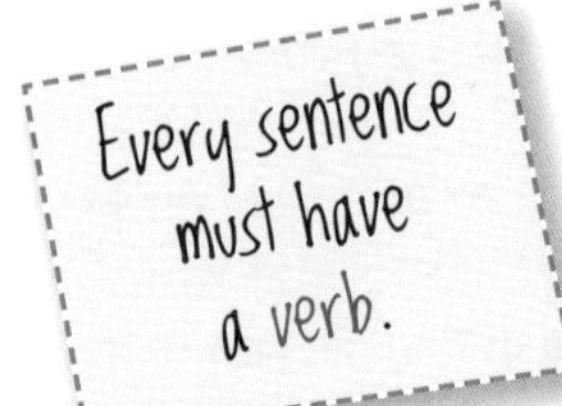
Every sentence must have a verb.

2

Draw pictures to show what these children are doing.

Ling plays hockey in the park.	Jeremy races his go-kart.	Diwan climbs up to his tree house.	Maddie feeds her pet fish.

3

Circle all the doing verbs in red.

The tennis ball bounced over the net.

Aneesh kicked the ball and scored another goal.

If I throw the ball, will you catch it?

The horse bucked, and the rider fell off.

When the phone rang, I ran inside and answered it.

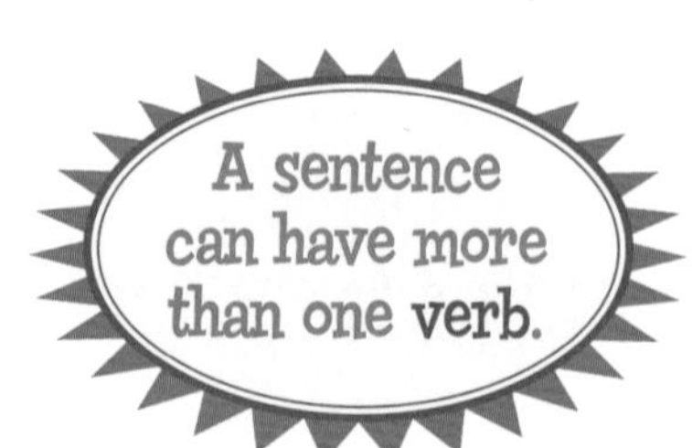
A sentence can have more than one verb.

VERBS

TARGETING GRAMMAR 3 © PASCAL PRESS ISBN 9781925076592

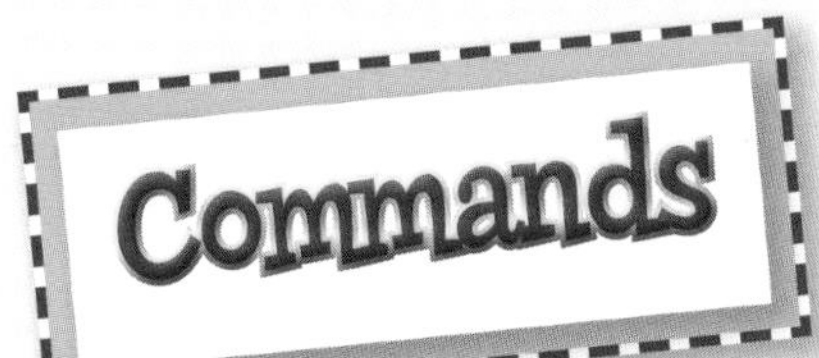

We use **commands** to *get things done*. They begin with a **doing verb**, e.g. **Shut** the gate. **Go** to bed. **Throw** the ball.

Circle the verbs in these commands.

Write your name at the top of the page.

Draw a picture of your favourite dessert.

Wash your hands before dinner, please.

Put your hands behind your back.

Meet me at the gate after school.

Two **commands** are often *joined by* **'and'**, e.g. **Go** and **play** outside. **Catch** the ball and **throw** it back to me.

Highlight the verbs in these commands.

Sit down and eat your lunch.

Clean your teeth and go to bed.

Feed the cat and take the dog for a walk, please.

Come and play cricket with me in the backyard.

Close the door and open the windows.

When a person is *not* to do something, place **do not** or the contraction **don't** *before* the verb, e.g. **Do not** swim outside the flags. **Don't** jump on the bed. **Don't** play in the mud.

Commands begin with a doing verb.

Change these commands from positive to negative.

Wait for me. ______________________

Throw the ball back. ______________________

Shut the door. ______________________

Open the window ______________________

'Saying' verbs show ***how people say*** things, e.g. Bill **said** I could come. Jessie **called** her friend. Tom **shouted** loudly.

1 Choose a suitable saying verb to complete each sentence.

laughed	screamed	called	asked	groaned	cried	whispered

"Would you like another cup of tea?" __________ David.

"Ha-ha-ha," ______________ Paul. "That was really funny."

"I've got a secret to tell you," __________________ Molly.

"EEEK!" _______________ Jill. "It's a mouse!"

"Oh, I may never see you again," _____________ Padma.

2 What do these animals 'say'?

dogs	squeak	wolves	chatter
roosters	trumpet	monkeys	neigh
mice	bark	frogs	howl
elephants	crow	horses	croak

3 Complete these sentences.

Jackson **said** that ____.

Dad **told** me to ____.

Mr Jones **asked** me ____.

4 Draw faces to illustrate these saying verbs.

giggle	sob	shout

TARGETING GRAMMAR 3 © PASCAL PRESS ISBN 9781925076592

Punctuation stop

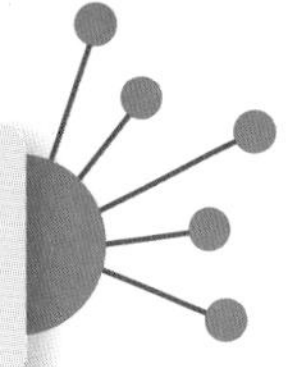

Writers mark their text to help readers make meaning. These marks are called **punctuation marks**.

Come and play cricket, Billy.

Okay, Matt. You can bat first.

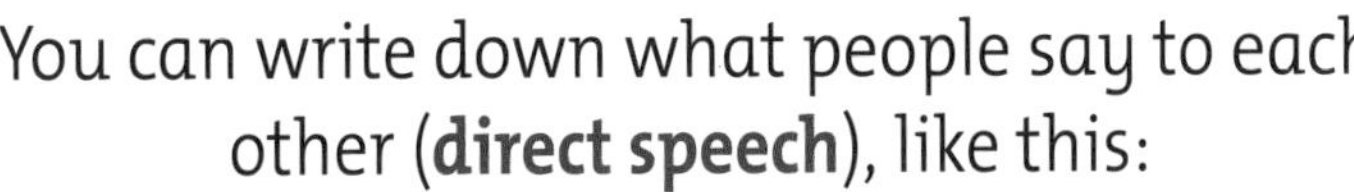

You can write down what people say to each other (**direct speech**), like this:

"Come and play cricket, Billy," said Matt.

"Okay, Matt. You can bat first," Billy said.

Just follow these simple steps:

1 Write down the **spoken words**.

2 Put **speech marks** around them (**" ... "**)

3 Always begin the first spoken word with a **capital letter**.

4 Put a **comma** between the speaker and their spoken words.

*NOTE: Use a '**?**' if the spoken words ask a question.*

Punctuate these sentences. *Hint: Highlight the spoken words first.*

Example: Sydney is our biggest city said James.

"Sydney is our biggest city," said James.

Dinner is ready Mum called.

Who would like a pizza asked Dad.

Paul said I think it will rain this afternoon.

I never get all my sums right Zara grumbled.

Eddie said I'm playing cricket on Saturday.

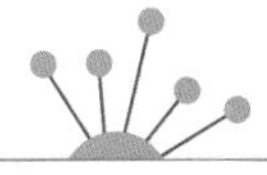

In a conversation, each new speaker begins on a new line.

"I can swim," said Jo.

"Me too," said Kay.

"I can't," said Jim.

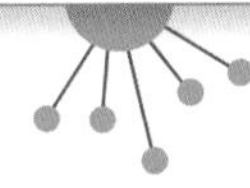

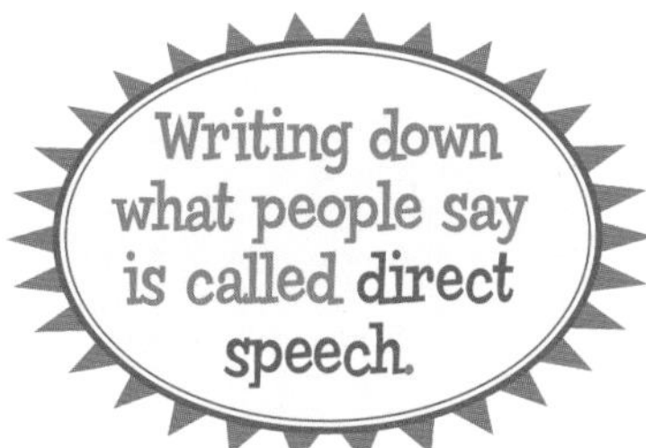

Writing down what people say is called direct speech.

VERBS

TARGETING GRAMMAR 3 © PASCAL PRESS ISBN 9781925076592

The **subject** says *who* or *what* is doing something. It is a **noun group** (or **pronoun**), e.g. **The man** plays golf.

In this sentence, it is '**The man**' who is playing, so 'The man' is the subject.

The verb is underlined. Circle the subject that says who or what is doing the action.

The Smith twins walk to school on Fridays.

Our class sang in the end-of-year concert.

They crossed the dry, sandy desert on camels.

Wild geese flew across high mountains on their way south.

The pipe band marched in the carnival parade.

2 Join the subject to the rest of the sentence.

Five little chicks	bounced high over the net.
Some of the students	blew the dark clouds away.
The tennis ball	hatched from the eggs.
The wind	grows cucumbers in his garden.
Mr Adams	play violins.

The subject is what a sentence is about.

Write sentences about these subjects.

A man wearing sunglasses ______________________________ .

The fishermen ______________________________ .

A clown ______________________________ .

Emma and Mark ______________________________ .

TARGETING GRAMMAR 3 © PASCAL PRESS ISBN 9781925076592

A **subject** and its **verb** must agree in number.
This means:
A **<u>singular subject</u>** has a **singular verb**,
e.g. The <u>fox</u> **hunts**. <u>The peach</u> **is** sweet.
A **<u>plural subject</u>** has a **plural verb**,
e.g. <u>The foxes</u> **hunt**. <u>The peaches</u> **are** sweet.

1 Choose the verb in the brackets that agrees with its subject.

Many children [go goes] to my school.

Bailey [run runs] to see the street parade.

Dad [drive drives] a big cattle truck.

Cows and kangaroos [drink drinks] at the waterhole.

Ben sometimes [wish wishes] he was older and taller.

2 Underline the mistake in each sentence. Write the correct word.

Fish swims in the sea. ______________________

A whale are a large sea animal. ______________________

Many boys rides their bikes to school. ______________________

My little sister like jelly and ice cream. ______________________

Babies cries when they are hungry. ______________________

The subject and its verb agree in number – both are singular or both are plural.

3 Add a subject to complete each sentence.

______________________________ live in water.

______________________________ crosses the street.

______________________________ fly across the sky.

______________________________ floats on water.

______________________________ swim in the sea.

TARGETING GRAMMAR 3 © PASCAL PRESS ISBN 9781925076592

Read this text and think about who or what each sentence is about – the subject.
Highlight the subject of each sentence.

PUPPETS

Puppets are doll-like figures of people or animals. They are operated by a person called a puppeteer (*pup-pet-ear*). The puppeteer uses his hands or strings to make the puppets move.

People have been making puppets for hundreds of years. They come in all shapes and sizes, and can be moved in many different ways by the puppeteer.

Finger puppets sit on the ends of the fingers. You can make a simple finger puppet by slipping a paper tube with a face drawn on it over your finger.

Glove puppets fit over the hands. You can make a simple glove puppet by sewing two buttons on an old sock and slipping it over your hand.

Rod puppets are much larger and are held up by wooden rods. Chinese festival dragons are usually rod puppets. They are controlled by people inside a dragon costume.

Shadow puppets are cardboard shapes with a stick attached. The puppeteer moves the puppet behind a screen with a light behind him. The people in front of the screen see only the black shapes of the puppets.

Marionettes (*marry-on-nets*) have jointed arms and legs. Strings are fastened to various parts of the body then attached to a control handle. The puppeteer can make the marionette move in very lifelike ways.

One of the most famous puppet plays is *Punch and Judy*. It has been performed for hundreds of years.

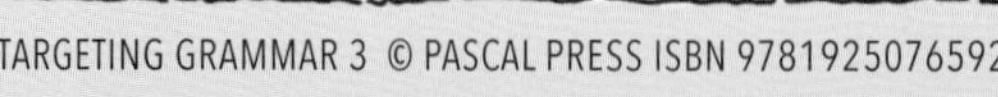
TARGETING GRAMMAR 3 © PASCAL PRESS ISBN 9781925076592

Many sentences have an **object**: someone or something that *receives the action* of the **subject**.

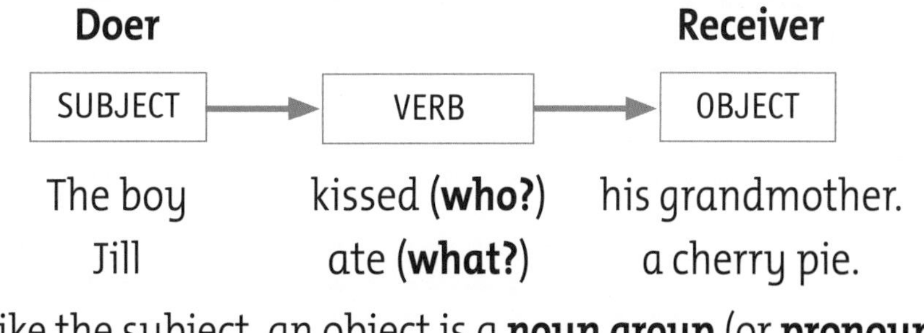

The boy	kissed (**who?**)	his grandmother.
Jill	ate (**what?**)	a cherry pie.

Like the subject, an object is a **noun group** (or **pronoun**).

1 Underline the objects of the bold actions in these sentences.

Mum **washes** the clothes in a washing machine.

I **read** an interesting book about rockets.

Dad **cooked** sausages on the barbecue.

I **lost** my ball, but Terry **found** it.

An excited crowd of people **are watching** the baseball game.

Ask 'who' or 'what' after the verb to find the object.

2 Tick only the sentences that have an object.
Hint: Find the verb first. Ask 'who' or 'what' to see if there is an object.

Mr Free bakes bread, pies and pastries. ☐

We hurried to the park to watch the fireworks. ☐

The chef threw the scraps in the bin. ☐

Not all the children wanted to go to the art gallery. ☐

Benson scored five goals in the first half of the game. ☐

3 Many sentences are structured (put together) in this way.

SUBJECT → VERB (doing) → OBJECT

The object receives the action of the subject.

Write two sentences using this structure.

(i) ____________________

(ii) ____________________

In a **command**, the **subject** is understood to be **'you'**, e.g. (You) Stay here. (You) Come with me. An **object** often follows the verb, e.g. Wipe **your feet**. Open **the gate**.

VERBS

Highlight the objects in these commands.

Put your schoolbooks in your bag.

Take the dog for a walk in the park, Tom.

Help your sister tie her shoelaces, please.

Please read your poem to the class, Molly.

Catch the ball then throw it back to me.

Here are the instructions for making a tasty toasted sandwich. Underline the objects.

1. Place a slice of bread on a board.
2. Spread mustard over the bread.
3. Put a slice of ham and a slice of cheese on top.
4. Place another slice of bread on top of the filling.
5. Melt some butter in a frying pan.
6. Cook the sandwich for three minutes on each side.
7. Lift the sandwich onto a plate.
8. Enjoy your snack!

Add an object to these commands. (Add any other words you need to complete your sentence.)

Close ____.

Wash ____.

Read ____.

Make ____.

Eat ____.

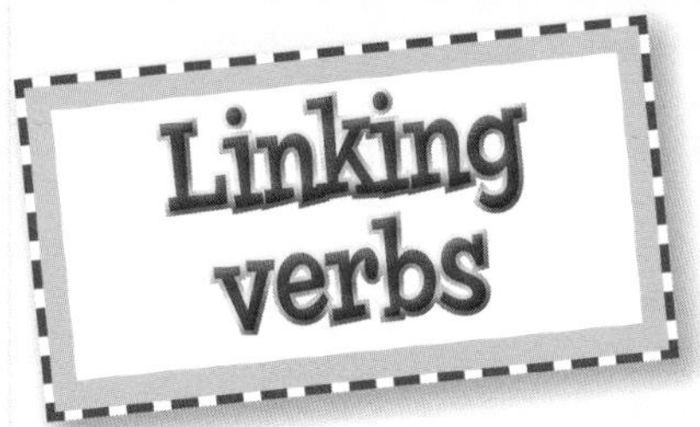

Linking verbs do not express action. They *connect ideas* about the **subject**, by describing it or renaming it, e.g. Jayde **is** a ballet dancer. Ahmed **was** late. He and I **are** good friends. Miss Tibbs **is** my teacher.

am is are was were

These verbs *always* link ideas together.
Think of them as an **equals sign (=)**.

VERBS

1 Complete the sentences using 'am', 'is' or 'are'.

A camel ________ an animal with a hump on its back.

Thomas ________ a champion swimmer.

I ________ a tall girl with long brown hair.

Where ________ my shoes?

One cat ________ black, and the other ________ white.

2 Circle the correct word in the brackets.

Jack [was were] at school early today.

There [was were] no room for me on the bus.

We [was were] glad to find our lost puppy.

Meg [was were] alone and afraid.

[Was Were] the sheep in their pens?

'be', **'being'** and **'been'** are also **linking verbs**, but must be used with another verb, e.g. I will **be** home soon. Gerry was **being** naughty. They have **been** awake since six o'clock.

3 Add the correct linking verb. Choose from 'be', 'being' and 'been'.

She will ___________ eight years old on Friday.

I have ___________ to the art gallery in Canberra.

They were just ___________ silly!

Have you ___________ to the Great Barrier Reef?

Jackson will ___________ the captain of our team.

A **verb group** has *more than one* **verb**, e.g.
Bill **can swim**. I **will wait** here. Tim **is eating** soup.
The last word in the group is the main word. The other words are called 'helping' or **auxiliary verbs**.

1 Underline the verb groups in these sentences.

Tilly is riding her black horse down a country lane.

A grasshopper can jump twenty times its length.

Jenny has fallen off her bike.

Some people are skating around the ice rink.

I will finish my book then I will go to bed.

VERBS

2 Draw a box around (i) the subject and (ii) the verb/verb group.

[Leo] [is running] across the playground.

The soldiers were marching down the street.

Jane can swim very well.

The two boys have been sliding in the mud.

We are waiting for the rain to stop.

The men have been fishing in the surf.

3 Illustrate the following sentences.

Mason **is riding** his bike.	The boys **are flying** kites.	Noah **can run** faster than Tom.
Emily **has been swimming.**	Ava **will buy** a blue hat.	Paul **was writing** a letter.

TARGETING GRAMMAR 3 © PASCAL PRESS ISBN 9781925076592

1 Highlight five verb groups in this story extract.

The sun was shining bright and warm over the little fishing village. The bay was catching the reflections of the tall ship in its still waters. Pietro and his friend, Erik, were sitting on the sea wall. They were watching the fishermen, who were bringing home their catch for the day.

"Let's go to the tavern for a mug of cider, Erik," Pietro said.

Amid the noise and clatter of the tavern, men were talking, eating and drinking. Several fishermen were sitting on high stools, the smell of fish still clinging to their hands. Sailors were drinking ale at a corner table.

"Hey, you sailors!" shouted a fisherman. "I hear you have been carrying treasure in that big ship of yours!"

2 Highlight five linking verbs in this story extract.

It was Friday. Bessie and May were in school. Just after lunch, a strong wind began to blow. A storm was coming. Thunder rolled in from the distance. Flashes of lightning lit up the classroom. Soon the storm was right over the school. Rain lashed the windows and ran down the gutters. The children listened to the wild storm raging above. Hail, the size of golf balls, pelted down. The teacher put a bucket under the leaking hole in the ceiling. No-one could hear over the noise on the roof. The storm went on for a very long time. It was very loud and a bit scary.

TARGETING GRAMMAR 3 © PASCAL PRESS ISBN 9781925076592

Verbs tell us *when* things are happening. **Tense** refers to the point in time they occur: in the present, in the past or in the future.

PRESENT:	Mum **bakes** cakes.	*(present tense)*
PAST:	Mum **baked** cakes.	*(past tense)*
FUTURE:	Mum **will bake** cakes.	*(future tense)*

 **Tick the box that shows the verb tense.**

	Present	Past	Future
Mr Riddle works in a shipping yard.	✓		
Stanley scored the first goal in the soccer match.			
I will meet my friends at the skate park.			
Robert plays both the violin and the piano.			
Dad washed his car on Saturday afternoon.			
A black brumby galloped through the wooded hills.			

 **Complete this table of singular present tense verbs.**

1st person	2nd person	3rd person
I paint	you paint	she paint**s**
I try	you ____________	it ____________
I ____________	you sneeze	he ____________
I wish	you wish	she ____________
I ____________	you hurry	he ____________

Add **'-s'** or **'-es'** to 3rd person verbs

TIP: Change **'y'** to **'i'** and add **'-es'**.

 **'-ed' is added to many verbs to show past tense. Complete this table.**

Present	walk	play	cry *	roll
Past	walk**ed**	____________	____________	____________
Present	trot *	hurry *	cook	stop *
Past	____________	____________	____________	____________

* Think about the spelling rules!

4 Add 'will' to the verb to show future tense.

I ____________ **meet** you at the park on Sunday.

All the students ____________ **go** to the museum by bus.

Mr Ellis ____________ **fly** to Perth on Monday.

____________ you **play** in the chess competition?

Helping verbs (auxiliary verbs) are part of a **verb group**. They work with **participles** to express *ongoing* or *continuous action*, either in the present or in the past.
He **is playing** football. ('continuous' **present tense**)
He **was playing** football. ('continuous' **past tense**)

'am', **'is'** and **'are'** are important **helpers**. They show things happening now in the *present*, e.g. **I am reading** a book. Fraser **is riding** an elephant. All the students **are wearing** hats.

VERBS

1 Add a helper to show something happening now.

These helpers work with **present participles (verb + -ing)**.

Robert ______ **playing** the violin.

Many people ______ **watching** the football game.

I ______ **training** for the school sports competition.

Bella ______ **walking** to school, but Jess ______ **riding** her bike.

Peter and Stuart ______ **collecting** mushrooms.

I ______ **going** to the beach on Sunday.

'was' and **'were'** are important **helpers**. They show things happening in the *past*, e.g. He **was eating** plums. They **were watching** TV.

Add a helper to show something happening in the past.

These helpers work with **present participles (verb + -ing)**.

The children _______ **collecting** seashells.

A red balloon ______ **floating** high above the rooftops.

Mrs Cherry _______ **conducting** the school choir.

All my friends ________ **waiting** for me at the school gate.

Thomas _______ **reading** a book about dragons.

Dark clouds _______ **gathering** in the west.

Present participles end in -ing.

TARGETING GRAMMAR 3 © PASCAL PRESS ISBN 9781925076592

'Have' verbs (has, have, having, had) express *ownership* or *action*, e.g. Once I **had** a cat, but now I **have** a dog. Bess **has** a bird. They **are having** a picnic.

VERBS

1 Add 'has', 'have', 'having' or 'had' to each sentence.

Sharks ____________ sharp teeth.

Cinderella ____________ nothing to wear to the ball.

I will ____________ lunch before I go for a walk.

We are ____________ a maths test on Friday.

Some dinosaurs ____________ small heads and very large bodies.

2 Choose the correct word in the brackets.

Evan [has have] a new mountain bike.

Kangaroos [has have] strong back legs and long tails.

Milly and her sister were [have having] a cup of tea.

Yesterday, John [has had] to leave early.

Joe [has have] a new house in the country.

'Have' verbs are also **helping verbs**.

3 Choose from 'has', 'have' or 'had' to complete these sentences.

Tom __________ **planted** beans and carrots in his garden.

__________ you **finished** your homework?

She __________ **painted** a picture of a mountain lake.

__________ Nathan **mowed** the lawn yet?

The children __________ never **played** softball before.

These helpers work with **past participles (regular verb + -ed)**.

Many past participles end in -ed

TARGETING GRAMMAR 3 © PASCAL PRESS ISBN 9781925076592

Regular verbs add endings to show **present** and **past tense**.

Add **-s** or **-es** *(3rd person present tense only)* He play**s**
Add **-ing** *(present continuous)* He is play**ing**
Add **-ing** *(past continuous)* He was play**ing**
Add **-ed** *(past tense)* He play**ed**

1 Add the correct ending to complete the verbs. Choose from -s, -es, -ing and -ed.

Billy is perform______ in the school concert next week.

He lift______ the lid to see what his mum was cook______ for dinner.

Ben always like______ to be first in line.

All Flynn want______ was a hot shower and a hot meal.

Harry watch______ TV every night. Do you?

A crowd of people was hurry______ to the Grand Final.

Irregular verbs have special **past tense forms**.

PRESENT I **ride** my bike. The wind **blows**.
Tom **runs** home.

PAST I **rode** my bike. The wind **blew**.
Tom **ran** home.

Write the past tense form of each word in the box.

slide	He ______________ down the slippery slide.
break	Who ______________ the window?
eat	Joe ______________ all the food on his plate.
write	Sarah ______________ a note to her friend.
drive	Dan ______________ his truck from Brisbane to Sydney.

Highlight the correct word in the brackets.

John [run ran] around the school oval.

The dog [stand stood] on his back legs.

Did you [know knew] the circus is in town?

The children [take took] their pets to school today.

The Jones family will [fly flew] to Japan on Friday.

Modal verbs are special helping verbs used to *express* a wide range of things such as ability, possibility, intention, permission and obligation, e.g. I **can** swim. You **must** do your work. I **will** love you forever!

Modal verbs			
can	will	should	may
could	would	must	might

1 Use modal verbs to complete these sentences.

Jan ____________ drive a car, but I can't.

I ____________ always like reading.

They ____________ go on their own if they were older.

You ____________ put on a seatbelt when you are in a car.

Mum ____________ let me go to the movies with you.

A **modal verb + not** expresses a *negative idea*, e.g. I **must not** cry. He **would not** wait for me. She **could not** swim. It is often expressed as a **contraction**, e.g. I **can't** sit there.

2 Write a contraction for each negative expression.

Lenny **would not** enter the dark cave. ____________

You **must not** jump on the bed. ____________

I **could not** see any planes in the sky. ____________

Jan **will not** come with us. ____________

You **should not** call people names. ____________

Modal verbs are used to make *requests*, e.g. **Will** you wait for me?

3 Add a modal verb to complete these requests.

____________ you play chess?

____________ I go now?

____________ you open your gift soon?

____________ you please stop chatting?

____________ you like to go to the football game?

TARGETING GRAMMAR 3 © PASCAL PRESS ISBN 9781925076592

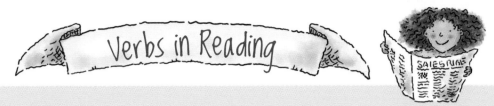

Verbs tell you what is 'going on' in a text: what the people and things are *doing*, *saying* or *being*. Action verbs bring a story to life, so you can picture what's happening in your head. When you read verbs like *twist*, *spin*, *crash*, *sizzle* and *plop*, you can really 'see' the action.

Read this story then illustrate it.

"Batten down the hatches! Secure the lifeboats," the captain shouted. His voice was torn away by the screaming wind. The storm finally hit the ship. Lightning split the sky in white-hot flashes of jagged light. The wind reached gale force, and rain lashed the decks. It was a monster of a storm, the likes of which the captain had never seen before. There was the screech of tearing metal as the funnel broke in half and crashed to the deck. It slammed into the railings and ripped them apart like matchsticks.

VERBS

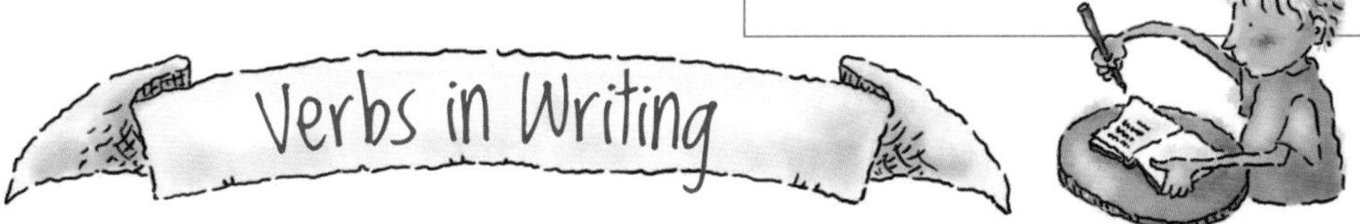

When you are writing a text, use **doing verbs** to show the *actions* of the people and things you are writing about. You can paint great pictures for your reader by using great **action verbs**.

In your notebook, write an ending to this story and illustrate it. Use some great action verbs.

Benson looked up to see a mountain looming above him. He pulled back hard on the control stick, and the helicopter rose steeply. He was almost clear of the mountain when he clipped the side and bent the blades. The helicopter began to spin downward, faster and faster...

Remember!

A capital letter begins a sentence.

A full stop ends a sentence. Commas separate words in a list.

TARGETING GRAMMAR 3 © PASCAL PRESS ISBN 9781925076592

VERBS Checkpoint ☑

VERBS

Circle eight action verbs and two saying verbs.

Suddenly, there is a noise like a big wind and the ground shakes violently.

"Quick, run! The volcano is about to blow!" shouts Benson. Bee and Benson run across the crater floor and over the rim. They slither down the mountainside. Behind them, the volcano explodes, sending ash high into the air.

"Faster!" yells Bee, as rocks begin to rain down on them and a river of hot lava spills from the crater. They stumble to the helicopter. Benson starts the engine, and the blades spin round and round. They lift to safety, just as the red fingers of hot lava reach the landing skids.

Circle the verb and underline the subject in each sentence.

The pirates hid the chest full of gold in a dark cave.
Deep underwater, the divers discovered the wreck of an old ship.
Freshwater crocodiles eat insects, fish, frogs, turtles and waterbirds.
The farmers have been harvesting their crops of wheat.
Oranges, lemons and mandarins are all citrus fruits.

Highlight the objects in these commands.

Cook two eggs in boiling water for three minutes.
Write your name at the top of the page.
Fill a bucket with warm, soapy water.
Eat two pieces of fruit every day.
Leave your homework on the teacher's table.

Punctuate this conversation.

You are late again says the teacher, glaring at Sam.
Sorry, Miss Tibbs mumbles Sam.
What's the reason this time she asks him with a sigh.
I missed the bus Sam mutters.
That's three times this week, Sam Miss Tibbs grumbles.

TARGETING GRAMMAR 3 © PASCAL PRESS ISBN 9781925076592

Highlight the correct verb in the brackets.

The miners [is are] deep underground.

[Has Have] you been to an art gallery?

I [do did] not go to the game on Sunday.

He has [being been] to see the dentist.

The people in the bus [was were] on their way to Darwin.

Tick the box that shows the verb tense.

	Present	Past	Future
Zeb will paint the fence brown.			
Bess made a yummy chocolate cake.			
Jeremy is training for the boxing match.			
I will buy Dad a book for his birthday.			
We had a picnic lunch by the river.			

Write the words in the box in past tense to complete the sentences.

float	The balloon ________________ in the air.
bite	That dog ________________ me!
blow	The wind ________________ the dark clouds away.
hide	The rabbit ________________ in the tall grass.
rest	The hikers ________________ after their long walk.

Choose a modal verb from the box to complete each sentence.

can	would	must	might	will

If I was rich, I ____________ buy a flashy red sports car.

____________ you come to my birthday party on Saturday?

Billy ____________ tap dance, but I can't.

You ____________ not swing on the clothesline!

Mum ____________ let me make biscuits today.

ADVERBS: Essentials

In this section, you will learn about the words that *say more* about **verbs**. These words are called **adverbs**.

Adverbs tell us *how*, *when* and *where* things happen.
Examples: The boys ran **quickly**. *(how)*
The boys ran in a marathon **yesterday**. *(when)*
The boys are **somewhere** *(where)* in the parklands.

Adverbs can also be used to ask **questions (How? When? Where? Why?)**.
Examples: **How** are you?
When will you go?
Where did you come from?
Why have you come?

An **adverbial phrase** is a group of words that does the same work as an adverb. **Adverbials** (**adverbs** and **adverbial phrases**) are the parts of a sentence that express *how*, *when*, *where* and *why* things are happening.

✤ TYPES OF ADVERBS	*Examples*
HOW **Adverbs of manner** tell you *how* something is happening.	He shouted **loudly**. She spoke **slowly**.
Many adverbs of manner are formed by adding **-ly** to an adjective.	slow**ly**, lazi**ly**, heavi**ly**, silent**ly**, happi**ly**, angri**ly**
An **adverbial phrase** can tell you *how* something is happening.	in a loud voice, with a smile, without looking, in an angry voice
WHEN **Adverbs of time** tell you *when* things are happening.	yesterday, tomorrow, sometimes, now
An **adverbial phrase** can tell you *when* something is happening.	on Friday, after school, before nightfall
WHERE **Adverbs of place** tell you *where* things are happening.	here, there, somewhere, away, nowhere, around
An **adverbial phrase** can tell you *where* something is happening.	in the park, at school, over the house, behind the door, on the table

When you see this sign, you can decide whether you want to challenge yourself!

TARGETING GRAMMAR 3 © PASCAL PRESS ISBN 9781925076592

Adverbs *say more* about verbs, e.g.
He spoke **softly**. The clouds are **high** in the sky.
I played tennis **yesterday**.

1 Adverbs tell us how something is happening. Circle the adverbs in these sentences.

Peter ran fast in the race and won.

He spoke loudly and angrily to the team.

He is training hard for the marathon.

Charlotte does her work well.

Cross the road quickly and carefully.

Find the **verb**. Ask *how* to find the **adverb**.

2 Adverbs tell us when or how often something is happening. Circle the adverbs in these sentences.

Serena always tries to do her best work.

We sometimes go to the Sunday market.

I will love you forever.

"See you later," Emily said.

Dinner will be ready soon.

Find the **verb**. Ask *when* or *how often* to find the **adverb**.

3 Adverbs tell us where something is happening. Circle the adverbs in these sentences.

Zac is hiding somewhere in the garden.

The dog ran away with his bone.

Here are my socks, and there are my shoes.

I can't find my hat anywhere.

Mum rocked the cradle backwards and forwards.

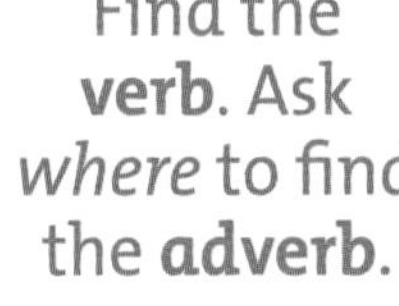

Find the **verb**. Ask *where* to find the **adverb**.

4 Circle the adverbs.

Zeb and Sam go BMX racing regularly. Yesterday, they were in a BMX race with three other boys. Zeb raced well and was soon in the lead. Sam lagged behind. At the last turn, Sam raced forward. He passed the others and won easily. He threw his arms triumphantly in the air.

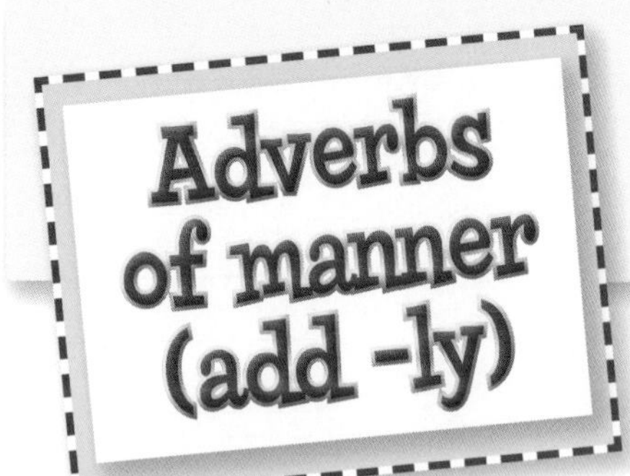

Adverbs of manner (add -ly)

Many **adverbs of manner** are made by adding **-ly** to an adjective, e.g. loud**ly**, soft**ly**, sad**ly**.

ADVERBS

1 Add -ly to these adjectives to make adverbs.

(Hint: Remember the 'y' rule!)

bright	______________	easy	______________
lazy	______________	secret	______________
local	______________	gentle	______________
careful	______________	helpful	______________

2 Choose an adverb from the list above to complete each sentence.

The cat stretched ______________ before the warm fireplace.

The sun shone ______________, and the wind blew ______________.

You should always cross a street ______________.

He can swim two lengths of the pool ______________.

Peaches and plums are grown ______________.

3 Choose the best adverb to complete each sentence. Colour the box beside it.

Thomas shouted ______________.

☐ angrily ☐ shyly ☐ softly

Last night, it snowed ______________.

☐ coldly ☐ heavily ☐ quickly

Mum folded the clothes ______________.

☐ roughly ☐ noisily ☐ neatly

David opened his gift ______________.

☐ recklessly ☐ eagerly ☐ sadly

TARGETING GRAMMAR 3 © PASCAL PRESS ISBN 9781925076592

Some **adverbs** are used to ask *questions*.
How are you?
When are we going to the beach?
Where are you going?
Why were you late for school?

1 Which adverbs would you use to ask these questions?

__________ are you going for your summer holiday?

__________ will dinner be ready?

__________ do you play Noughts and Crosses?

__________ aren't you wearing your hat?

ADVERBS

2 Answer these questions.

Where do you go to school? ____________________

How many toes do you have? ____________________

When is your birthday? ____________________

Why does an ant have feelers? ____________________

3 Circle the correct adverb in the brackets.

[When How] do you make popcorn?

[Where When] have you been?

[Where Why] are you laughing?

[Where How] were you playing Hide and Seek?

[When Why] does the library open?

How?, When?, Where? and Why? are good questions to ask when researching a topic.

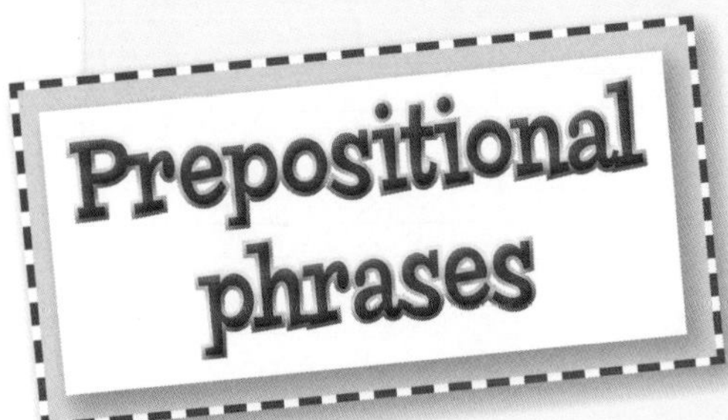

A **phrase** is a group of words *without* a verb.
It is often introduced by a **preposition** and is called a **prepositional phrase**.
A **prepositional phrase** does the work of an:
(i) **adjective** (adjectival phrase) *The girl* ***in a pink dress.***
(ii) **adverb** (adverbial phrase) *He ran* ***across the sand.***

1 Write some prepositional phrases.

____
____
____
____
____
____
____
____

about	*behind*	*from*	*through*
above	*below*	*in*	*till*
across	*beneath*	*into*	*to*
after	*beside*	*near*	*towards*
against	*between*	*of*	*under*
along	*by*	*off*	*until*
almost	*down*	*on*	*up*
around	*during*	*over*	*upon*
at	*except*	*past*	*with*
before	*for*	*since*	*without*

2 Choose a preposition to complete each adverbial phrase.

Wipe the glasses ______________ **a soft cloth.**
Ants are crawling ______________ **the kitchen bench.**
It rained heavily ______________ **the night.**
My dog, Jasper, walks ______________ **me.**
Did you look ______________ **the shed?**
I feed my pets ______________ **school.**
Do not run ______________ **the street.**
Harry dived ______________ **the waves.**

Prepositional phrases can do the work of adverbs.

3 Add the missing prepositions.

The Great Wall of China is an amazing 7300 km long and is more than 2000 years old. It runs ______________ east to west along the border ______________ China and Mongolia. It crosses steep mountains and deep valleys. The Wall is made _________ earth, brick, wood and stone. It was built entirely __________ hand and is one _________ the great wonders ________ the world.

TARGETING GRAMMAR 3 © PASCAL PRESS ISBN 9781925076592

Adverbial phrases say *how*, *when*, *where* and *why* things happen.
Terry answered **with a smile**. *(how)*
Jan has a piano lesson **after school**. *(when)*
We went **to the beach** *(where)* **for a swim**. *(why)*

What do the adverbial phrases say about the verb?

	How	When	Where	Why
On Sunday, we will drive **to the South Coast**.		✓	✓	
After school, we will buy a gift **for mum's birthday**.				
With great care, she placed the kitten **in the basket**.				
We don't play **in the yard** **on wet days**.				
I went **to the shop** **for an ice cream**.				
At school, we do maths **in the morning**.				

Choose an adverbial phrase from the box to complete each sentence.

into the pool	during the storm	in ten minutes
with a soft cloth	for his bravery	on the stove
below the waves	after the party	under a log

The train will depart ______________________. (When?)

He polished his shoes ______________________. (How?)

A spear fisherman dived ______________________. (Where?)

The soldier received a medal ______________________. (Why?)

______________________ a tree fell across the power lines. (When?)

An adverbial phrase usually begins with a preposition.

Finish these sentences.

During the holidays, I ______________________.

At school, I ______________________.

With a cheerful smile, I ______________________.

ADVERBS

CHALLENGE

An **adverbial** (**adverb** or **adverbial phrase**) is the part of a sentence that tells you *how*, *when*, *where* or *why* things are happening.

Underline five more adverbials in this extract from *Kokoda Sunrise*.

Mangivar dragged the wounded soldier off the track. He covered him with fern leaves. This would hide him from the enemy and keep him a little warmer.

The soldier whispered, "I must warn the other soldiers that the enemy are somewhere nearby."

"I'll take a message to them, and I'll bring someone back to help you," Mangivar said bravely.

The soldier reached into his pocket. He took out a faded photo and the stub of a pencil. He wrote some words on the back of the photo and handed it to Mangivar.

"Please... take this photo back to the army camp and give it to the captain. He will know what to do."

TARGETING GRAMMAR 3 © PASCAL PRESS ISBN 9781925076592

Verbs tell you what is happening in a text. **Adverbs** and **adverbial phrases** tell you *how*, *when*, *where* and *why* these things are happening. When you read a story, these **adverbials** tell you what place you are in and what time of day it is. They tell you *how* and *why* people are doing and saying things. This helps you to picture what is happening in your head.

ADVERBS

Read this text then draw a picture.

A sudden gust of wind swooped through Geraldine's window. It lifted up her precious model plane and sent it gliding around the room. The plane bumped against her T-Rex, tipping it off the shelf. As the dinosaur crashed to the floor, it hit the side of her tall ship, sending it sliding off the table. Both ended in splinters on the floor. Geraldine Georgina Jones gaped at the mess.

When you are writing a text, use **adverbs** and **adverbial phrases** to *say more* about the actions of the people and things you are writing about. Use them to show *how*, *when* or *where* things are happening.

In your notebook, write a few sentences about what you did during your last holiday. Begin by saying when it was. Ask a friend to read your story and draw a picture.

A **capital letter** begins a sentence.
A **full stop** ends a sentence.
Commas separate words in a list.

TARGETING GRAMMAR 3 © PASCAL PRESS ISBN 9781925076592

ADVERBS Checkpoint ☑

Highlight the adverbs and adverbial phrases.

Two boys raced along the beach, their kites flapping merrily in the wind. A dog yapped playfully at their heels and sent the sand crabs scuttling. Waves crashed onto the rocks and threw spray high into the air. It hung there like a rainbow.

2 Add prepositions to complete the sentences.

Put the cake ________ the oven.

Wipe your hands ________ this towel.

He stood with his hands __________ his back.

A black horse trotted ________ the road.

Dad leaned the ladder __________ the wall ________ the house.

3 Underline the adverbial phrases. Then write whether they tell you 'how', 'when', 'where' or 'why'.

Last night, the moon was hidden by clouds.

when how

On warm summer days, we love to go swimming in the pool.

____

At the toy shop, Mum bought a skateboard for me.

____

In the morning, we are going to the beach for a holiday.

____

4 Complete the questions using 'how', 'when', 'where' or 'why'.

__________ is the football stadium?

__________ will I see you again?

__________ do you make pancakes?

__________ are the children not wearing hats?

TARGETING GRAMMAR 3 © PASCAL PRESS ISBN 9781925076592

SENTENCES: Essentials

In this section, you will learn about **sentences**. A sentence is a 'chunk' of words built around one complete thought. We use sentences to make **statements**, ask **questions** or give **commands**. A sentence is the most important building block in our language.

A sentence can be long or short, and always has a **verb**.

Examples: I **like** pizza. **Go** away! Who **is** he?
Today, our class **is going** on a trip to the museum to see the dinosaurs.

✤ TYPES OF SENTENCES	*Examples*
Statements *tell* you things. They start with a **capital letter** and end with a **full stop (.)**.	**I** came first in my race**. D**ad drives a big truck**. M**y teacher is Miss Hunt**.**
Questions *ask* for things and want answers. They start with a **capital letter** and end with a **question mark (?)**.	**W**hat's for dinner**? W**here is my hat**?** **M**ay I ride your bike**?**
Commands *demand* that something be done. They start with a **capital letter** and end with a **full stop (.)**. Commands usually begin with a **verb**. They can be polite. (See *Verbs* pp. 57 & 64)	**Cut** around the picture. **Bring** your lunch and a hat. **Close** the door, please.
Exclamations *express* strong feelings like surprise, fear, excitement or anger. They start with a **capital letter** and end with an **exclamation mark (!)**.	**H**elp**! G**o away**! W**ow**! S**tand back everybody**!**
Simple sentences A **simple sentence** expresses *one thought*. It has one **subject** and one **verb** (or verb group).	The bird **flew** away. The children **are playing** handball.
Compound sentences A **compound sentence** is made up of two simple sentences *joined* by a **joining word (and, but, or** and **so)**.	It is late **and** it is getting dark. I called his name, **but** he didn't hear me.

The **subject** tells you *who* or *what* the **sentence** is about.

A sentence may contain an **object** (the one that receives the action of the subject) and/or an **adverbial** (adverb or adverbial phrase).

Examples:

Cinderella	**lost**	her slipper.
(subject)	(verb)	(object)

A long black snake	**slithered**	across the road.
(subject)	(verb)	(adverbial)

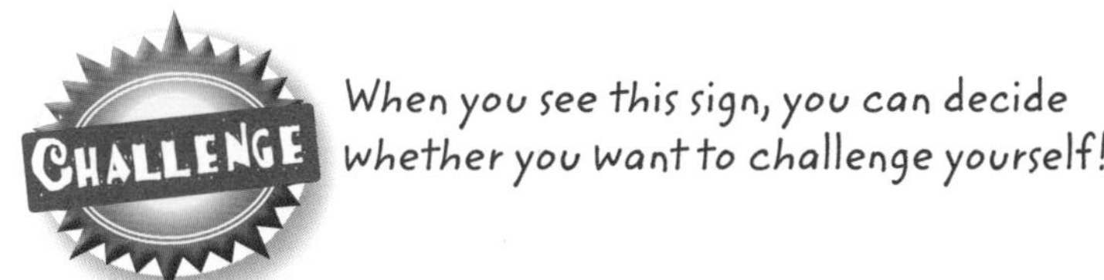

When you see this sign, you can decide whether you want to challenge yourself!

We express our thoughts, one at a time, in **sentences**. The *beginning* of each sentence is marked by a **capital letter**. The end is marked by a **full stop (.)**, an **exclamation mark (!)** or a **question mark (?)**.

An owl is a big bird with two large round eyes**.**

Look out**!**

What are you doing**?**

Some sentences make **statements**. We **state** (say) what we think and how we feel. We *begin* with a **capital letter** and *end* with a **full stop**.

SENTENCES

Write a statement about each picture.

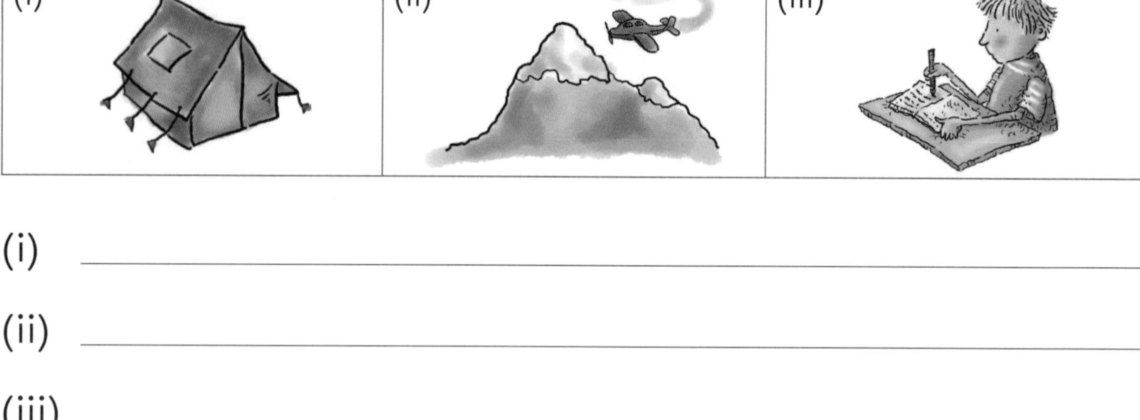

(i) ____________________

(ii) ____________________

(iii) ____________________

Use capital letters and full stops to punctuate the sentences.

gold is easy to shape because it is soft it can be beaten into paper-thin sheets or stretched into fine wire gold will only melt at very high temperatures it will not rust or tarnish these qualities make it a long-lasting metal of great beauty

every day at sunset, a pesky fox comes prowling around the henhouse disturbing our chooks the chooks cluck and cackle and scramble back to the safety of their perches there are feathers everywhere, and the chooks have stopped laying eggs dad says something has to be done

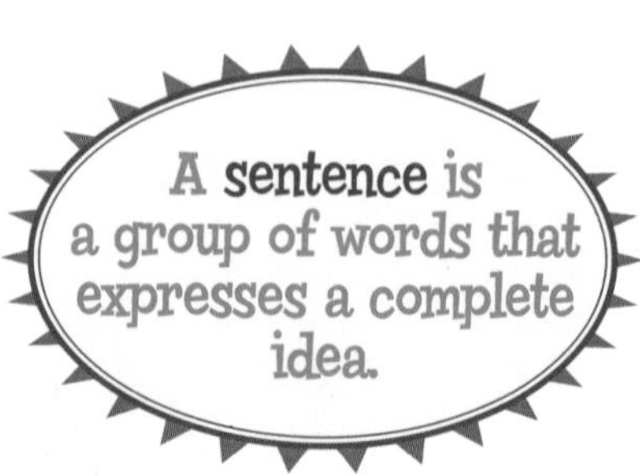

A sentence is a group of words that expresses a complete idea.

TARGETING GRAMMAR 3 © PASCAL PRESS ISBN 9781925076592

A sentence has a **subject**. It is *who* or *what* the sentence is about. The subject is a **noun group** or a **pronoun**, e.g. **That book** is mine. **Jack and Jill** went up the hill. **The man in the red shirt** is the captain.

1 Underline the subject of each sentence.

This shy and unusual animal is called a platypus.

A man on a motorbike went past my house.

After school, we will go to football training.

Peaches, plums and apricots are all stone fruits.

Here is a basket of bread.

SENTENCES

Subject-verb agreement

The **subject** and **verb** *agree* in **number**. This means that a **singular subject** has a **singular verb** and a **plural subject** has a **plural verb**.

The boy **rides** his bike.	The boys **ride** their bikes.
The cat **sleeps**.	The cats **sleep**.
The dog **is barking**.	The dogs **are barking**.

2 Choose the verb from the brackets that agrees with each subject.

The horses [was were] galloping across the grassy plains.

The children [has have] tickets to the circus.

Dad always [close closes] the windows at night.

The weary traveller [has have] gone to sleep in his tent.

Jonathan Fox [is are] interested in science.

3 Put a red box around the subject and a blue box around the verb.

Jackson and his two friends are riding their horses in a horse show.

She has been swimming in the school pool.

The men in the boxing ring are wearing padded leather gloves.

Several of the fishermen caught large tuna fish.

After the storm, leaves and branches littered the streets.

The **subject** is *who* or *what* the sentence is about.

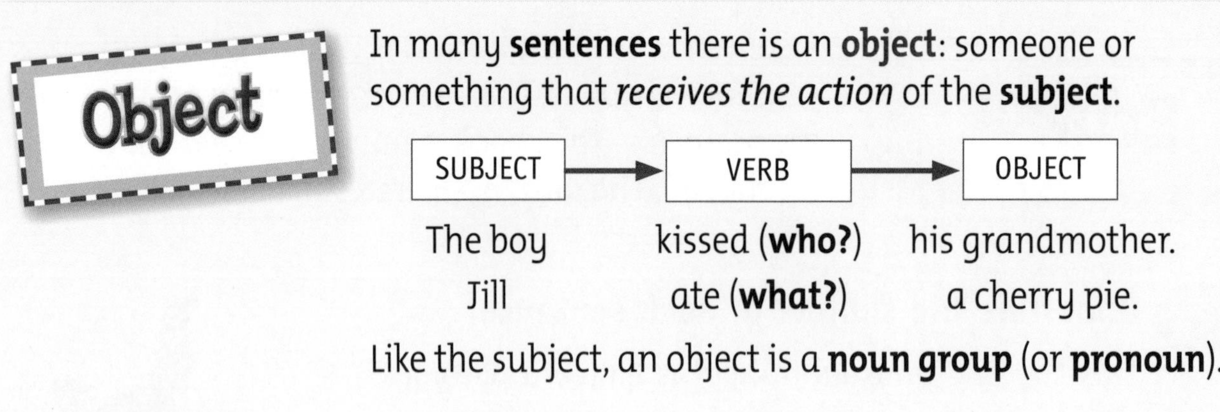

Object

In many **sentences** there is an **object**: someone or something that *receives the action* of the **subject**.

SUBJECT → VERB → OBJECT

The boy	kissed (**who?**)	his grandmother.
Jill	ate (**what?**)	a cherry pie.

Like the subject, an object is a **noun group** (or **pronoun**).

Underline the objects of the actions in these sentences.

We bought fairy floss at the show.

Jason ate a packet of potato chips.

A camel train crossed the hot, sandy desert.

Please leave your shoes at the back door.

Mum made a chocolate cake with pink icing for my birthday.

Ask who or what after the verb to find the object.

Tick only those sentences that contain an object.
Hint: Find the verb first. Ask 'who' or 'what' to see if there is an object.

Elephants have a long trunk and long ivory tusks. ☐

My sister and I offered to wash Dad's car. ☐

Dan will buy oranges, apples and bananas. ☐

Mum heated the custard in the microwave. ☐

Scones are baked in a hot oven. ☐

In these sentences, put a box around the subject in red, the verb in blue and the object in green. *Hint: Find the verb first.*

The angry giant snapped the branch with his bare hands.

Each of the kids in my class made an animal out of clay.

Jack and Jill took the pail of water to the bottom of the hill.

We rode our horses along the grassy hills above the city.

The man in the yellow life jacket paddled his kayak down the river.

The **object** is who or what receives the action of the **subject**.

TARGETING GRAMMAR 3 © PASCAL PRESS ISBN 9781925076592

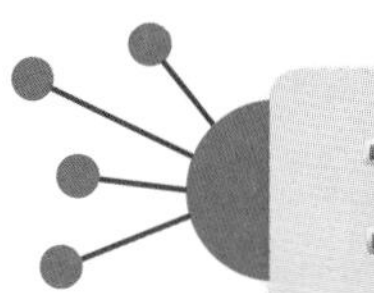

Building statements

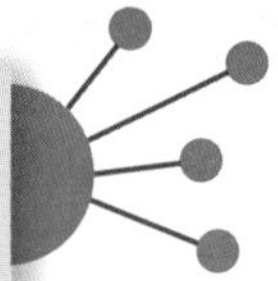

Build statements using these simple frameworks.

SUBJECT (noun group or pronoun)	VERB (verb or verb group)	OBJECT (noun group or pronoun)
The chef	is baking	buns, pies and cakes.
....	is writing	....
....	....	a glass of lemonade.
....	are playing	....

SUBJECT (noun group or pronoun)	VERB (verb or verb group)	ADVERBIAL (adverb or adverbial phrase)
A crowd of people	is waiting	for the bus.
....	cycled	....
....	....	along the beach.
....	went	....

SUBJECT (noun group or pronoun)	VERB (verb or verb group)	OBJECT (noun group or pronoun)	ADVERBIAL (adverb or adverbial phrase)
Tania	hung	her hat	on a peg.
....	lost	....	....
Yuki	....	his books	....
....	is cooking	....	....

④

ADVERBIAL (adverb or adverbial phrase)	SUBJECT (noun group or pronoun)	VERB (verb or verb group)	ADVERBIAL (adverb or adverbial phrase)
At the weekend	we	are going	to the beach.
....	....	swam	....
Sometimes	....	....	....
....	....	play	....

SENTENCES

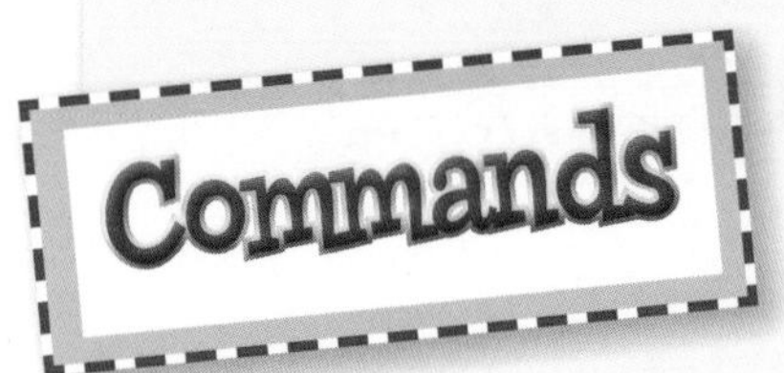

Some sentences are **commands**. The **subject** of a command is always '*you*'. Some commands have <u>objects</u> and some don't. A command begins with a **doing verb**, e.g. **Wait** for me. **Shut** <u>the door</u>. **Stand** up tall. **Wash** <u>your face</u>.

Circle the verbs in these commands.

Please read me a story before bed.

Open the can and empty the soup into a saucepan.

Put your hands behind your back and don't touch anything.

Whip the cream and add some sugar.

Always swim between the flags.

Highlight any objects in these commands.

Run and **hide** behind the shed in the garden.

Snap your fingers and **click** your heels.

Boil the potatoes in a saucepan.

Please **handle** this old vase with great care.

Go away and **don't bother** me!

Commands tell '*you*' to do something.

Exclamations are sentences where people suddenly cry out in *fright*, *anger* or *surprise*. These sentences end in an **exclamation mark**, e.g. Stop**!** Help me**!** Get out of the way**!**

Draw pictures to match the exclamations.

Oh no! I've lost my hat again!	Wow! What a gift! Thank you!	You won the marathon? That's awesome!

TARGETING GRAMMAR 3 © PASCAL PRESS ISBN 9781925076592

Some sentences ask **questions**. They end in a **question mark**, e.g. **What** is her name**?** **Where** do crocodiles live**?** **Who** won the game**?**

1 Add a word to complete these questions.

_______ was the Eiffel Tower built?

_______ old is the Great Wall of China?

_______ do frogs change their colours?

_______ discovered Australia?

_______ city is the capital?

_______ is a Brontosaurus?

We often *split* the **verb group** to ask a question, e.g. **Are** you **going** to the beach today? **Do** you **like** pizza? **Have** you **been** to Tasmania?

2 Rewrite these statements as questions.

Dan **will go** to the beach today.

______________________________?

You **have seen** this movie before.

______________________________?

They **would like** pancakes and syrup.

______________________________?

We **can go** for a swim in the pool later.

______________________________?

Tag questions are statements with a **tag** on the end. We use tags to *check our thoughts* with someone, e.g. I like playing chess, **don't you**? You don't like me, **do you**?

3 Add a tag to ask a question.

You do have a hat, ____________________?

You won't be long, ____________________?

They don't have any money, ____________________?

You can swim, ____________________?

Your brother isn't very happy, ____________________?

A comma always comes before a tag.

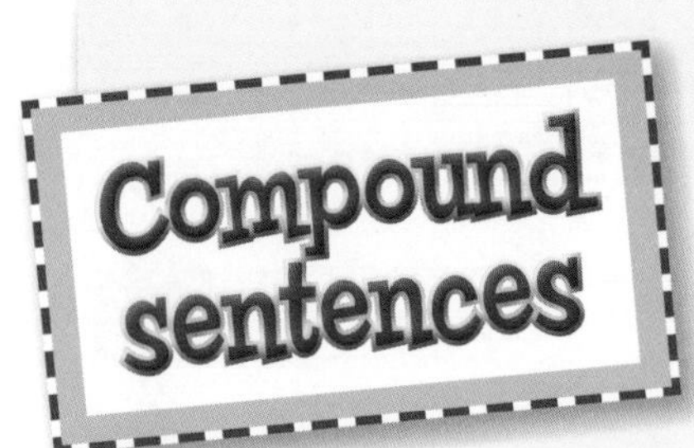

Compound sentences are two **simple sentences** *joined together* with a **joining word**, e.g. I like apples **and** I like bananas. My face is clean, **but** my hands are dirty.

Joining words: **and** **so** **but** **or**

SENTENCES

1 Join the sentences with a joining word. Choose from 'and', 'so', 'but' and 'or'.

Sometimes we play cricket ________ sometimes we play baseball.

It is late ________ I must leave.

You can eat it now ________ leave it until later.

Put the eggs in a pot ________ boil them for three minutes.

Tom shouted loudly ________ no-one heard him.

Stay on the path ________ you might get lost.

2 Colour the correct joining word in the brackets.

Jess wants to go to the pool [and but] she can't swim.

We got on our bikes [so and] rode to the lake.

I bought a chocolate frog [but and] gave it to Jack.

We can walk to school [or but] we can go by bus.

I'll get my bike [or so] I can ride with you.

Jessie had five dollars [but so] she lost it.

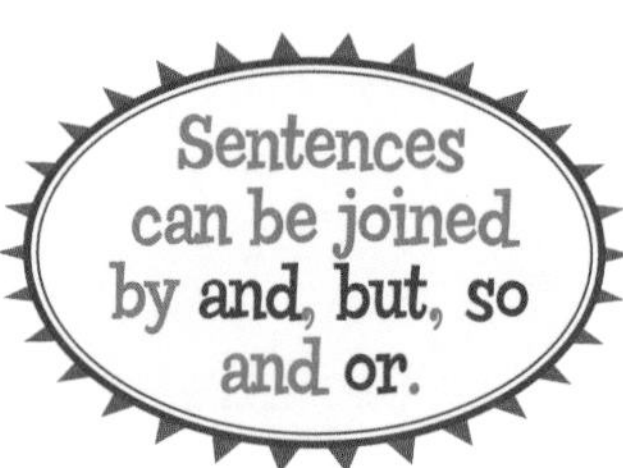

Sentences can be joined by and, but, so and or.

3 Join the sentences together with a joining word.

You can have an apple pie		he could buy a model plane.
There's room in our car	**and**	the tanks are full.
I eat lettuce	**but**	you can have a cream bun.
It rained heavily last night	**so**	his dad won't let him.
Ken would like to come	**or**	I don't like cucumber.
Zeb saved his money		you can come with us.

TARGETING GRAMMAR 3 © PASCAL PRESS ISBN 9781925076592

Subject

Each part of a **compound sentence** has a **subject**.
Sometimes the subjects are the same and sometimes they are different.
I am feeling hot, so **I** will switch on the fan. *(same)*
I am leaving now, and **Casey** is coming with me. *(different)*

1 Underline the joining word in each compound sentence then circle the subjects. Write whether the subjects are the same or different.

They waited for twenty minutes, but the bus didn't come. ____________

Dad lifted me onto his shoulders, so I could see the parade. ____________

I would like to make pancakes, but I don't know how. ____________

You must hurry, or you will miss the bus. ____________

Sally will wash the dishes, and Bo will dry them. ____________

If the **subject** in each part of the sentence is the *same*, the second subject is often replaced by a **pronoun**, or left out altogether.
Mary is younger than me, but **she** is taller.
Jake hurt his leg, so **he** can't play cricket.
I will go to the shop and buy an ice cream.

2 Are the subjects the same (S) or different (D) in these compound sentences?

We were going to the park, **but** it began to rain. ____________

Maree bought a toffee apple **and** gave it to Jimmy. ____________

Josh kicked the penalty goal, **and** his team won. ____________

Put that dollar in your pocket, **or** you might lose it! ____________

I turned up the heat, **and** the potatoes boiled over. ____________

Terry had a pet budgie, **but** it flew away. ____________

Gus hasn't got a ticket, **so** he can't go to the game. ____________

Tess likes jigsaw puzzles, **but** Tina likes board games. ____________

SENTENCES

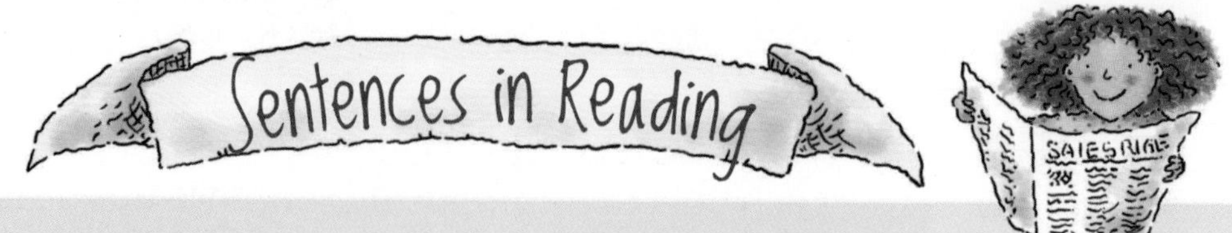

A text is built **sentence** by sentence, one idea after another. Most sentences end in a **full stop** to show that an idea is complete. Stop at a full stop before reading on! **Commas** are used within sentences to show which words should be read together. Take a small break when you see a comma before reading on! Remember, the punctuation marks are there to help readers understand a text more easily.

SENTENCES

Read this text, sentence by sentence, and draw a picture.

A rainbow is an arc of colour across the sky. It is a wonderful and almost magical thing, because it is not 'real' like rain or snow. We can see it, but we can't touch it. We can chase it, but we can't catch it. You usually see rainbows after storms, when the sun shines and the air is still filled with raindrops. White sunlight shines through the raindrop, and is reflected from the inside of each drop. The light splits into bright bands of colour — red, orange, yellow, green, blue, indigo and violet.

You write a text **sentence** by sentence. Start with your first idea and put it in a sentence. Your next idea is your next sentence. Each sentence you write adds another idea to the ones you have already written.

In your notebook, write a sentence about an animal. Begin by saying what it is. Then add three or four more sentences about that animal. Draw a picture of your animal. Ask a friend to read what you've written.

Sentences begin with capital letters.
They end in full stops, question marks or exclamation marks.
Commas show breaks between words.

TARGETING GRAMMAR 3 © PASCAL PRESS ISBN 9781925076592

Write a statement or question about each picture.

(i) ______________________________

(ii) ______________________________

(iii) ______________________________

(iv) ______________________________

(v) ______________________________

What are these sentences about? Underline the subject.

Many tourists travel to America to visit New York.

Cricket balls and cricket bats are on sale at the sports shop.

Unfortunately, our team lost the football game on Friday.

Jason has lost the key to the front door.

A girl wearing a hat and sunglasses strolled along the sand.

Circle the objects in these commands.

Put the jelly in the fridge to set.

Lock all the doors and windows, please.

Don't bounce your ball in the house.

Shuffle the cards and deal them out.

Write your name and address on the back of the envelope.

 **Highlight the correct verb in the brackets.**

The twins [go goes] to the library every day.

Marty and her brothers [is are] playing darts.

Giraffes [has have] long necks and long legs.

Jack [play plays] with his Lego blocks.

I have [did done] my homework.

 **Add a joining word to complete these compound sentences.**

Jackson is fast ________ he's not as fast as Billy.

Jamie raced along the beach ________ his dog followed him.

I like oranges ________ I don't like lemons.

Ben had no money ________ he couldn't buy anything.

You'll have to run fast ________ you won't catch me.

6 **Mark the capital letters, commas, apostrophes and full stops in this text.**

oranges lemons and limes are citrus fruits grown in australia grapefruit mandarins and cumquats are also citrus fruits citrus fruits have orange yellow or green skins the soft pulp inside is divided into sections most citrus fruits contain seeds

most of australias citrus crops are oranges a large part of each years crop goes into the making of juice some oranges are made into a jam called marmalade

7 **If a genie granted you three wishes, what would they be? Write about your three wishes in sentences.**

____

____

____

____

____

____

TARGETING GRAMMAR 3 © PASCAL PRESS ISBN 9781925076592